Graphic Novels in High School and Middle School Classrooms

Graphic Novels in High School and Middle School Classrooms

A Disciplinary Literacies Approach

William Boerman-Cornell
Jung Kim
Michael L. Manderino

ROWMAN & LITTLEFIELD
Lanham • Boulder • New York • London

Published by Rowman & Littlefield
A wholly owned subsidiary of The Rowman & Littlefield Publishing Group, Inc.
4501 Forbes Boulevard, Suite 200, Lanham, Maryland 20706
www.rowman.com

Unit A, Whitacre Mews, 26-34 Stannary Street, London SE11 4AB

British Library Cataloguing in Publication Information Available

Library of Congress Cataloging-in-Publication Data

Names: Boerman-Cornell, William, 1966– author. | Kim, Jung, 1977– author. | Manderino, Michael, author.
Title: Graphic novels in high school and middle school classrooms : a disciplinary literacies approach / William Boerman-Cornell, Jung Kim, Michael L. Manderino.
Description: Lanham, Maryland : Rowman & Littlefield, [2017] | Includes bibliographical references.
Identifiers: LCCN 2017010196 (print) | LCCN 2017010595 (ebook) | ISBN 9781475828344 (hardback : alk. paper) | ISBN 9781475828351 (pbk. : alk. paper) | ISBN 9781475828368 (electronic)
Subjects: LCSH: Graphic novels in education. | Graphic novels—Study and teaching. | Comic books, strips, etc., in education. | Comic books, strips, etc.—Study and teaching. | Literacy.
Classification: LCC LB1044.9.C59 B64 2017 (print) | LCC LB1044.9.C59 (ebook) | DDC 371.33—dc23
LC record available at https://lccn.loc.gov/2017010196

∞ ™ The paper used in this publication meets the minimum requirements of American National Standard for Information Sciences Permanence of Paper for Printed Library Materials, ANSI/NISO Z39.48-1992.

Printed in the United States of America

Contents

Foreword

In today's challenging educational climate, it can be difficult for teachers to find ways to engage and motivate reluctant young readers. Scripted curricula, district mandates, and state and national standards seem to constrain opportunities for expanding the kinds of texts that are used in the classroom. Despite these constraints, we know that many youth and young people are strongly drawn to visual narratives that provide mirrors, windows, and doors into their own experiences, as well as those of others (Sims Bishop, 1990). From fan work on social media sites like Tumblr to superhero movies at the box office, stories told through images draw audiences of all ages. Capturing the excitement that many students experience while engaged in participatory graphics outside the classroom has heretofore been akin to catching lightning in a bottle, demonstrating the need for best practices at the convergence of visual literacies, multimodality, interdisciplinary teaching, and social justice.

In *Graphic Novels in High School and Middle School Classrooms: A Disciplinary Literacies Approach*, William Boerman-Cornell, Jung Kim, and Michael L. Manderino provide teaching tools that are timely and relevant for a new generation of teachers and students. The unique contribution of this book is that it extends the teaching of graphic novels beyond reading, literacy, and language arts to encompass the entire curriculum. Not only do the authors provide clarity about the role of disciplinary literacy and define the genre and terminology of graphic novels, they also provide classroom-ready strategies and tips for humanities and STEM subjects in secondary schools. The concept of picture-text hybridity can help teachers select and evaluate graphic novels for whole-class units, small-group instruction, and individualized perusal from the classroom library. Chapters on using graphic novels for inquiry across the disciplines complete the volume.

One of the greatest affordances of *Graphic Novels in High School and Middle School Classrooms* is that it encourages teachers and their students to move toward the "unflattening" of texts advocated by comics scholar Nick Sousanis in his groundbreaking 2015 text. Moving beyond Scott McCloud's essential work in *Understanding Comics* (1993), Sousanis notes, "Traditionally, words have been privileged as the proper mode of explanation, as *the* tool of thought. Images have, on the other hand, long been sequestered to the realm of spectacle and aesthetics, sidelined in serious discussions as mere illustrations to support the text—never as equal partner" (Sousanis, 2015, p. 54). By focusing on the ways that graphic novels can be used to support instruction in disciplinary literacies, the authors of this book you are holding have provided an essential intervention in reading across the curriculum. Given that texts in the disciplines often require multimodal literacy, and that meaning is often made through semiotics other than language, *Graphic Novels in High School and Middle School Classrooms* provides a visual grammar that is both accessible and practical.

Another contribution of *Graphic Novels in High School and Middle School Classrooms* is its conclusion. Often, comics and graphic novel teaching volumes provide far more information about the topic than is useful for busy classroom teachers. Each chapter is grounded in theory, provides practical applications, and can immediately be used for planning effective classroom instruction.

Now more than ever, it is vital to find ways to engage adolescent readers and to teach them how to critically deconstruct the image-laden narratives that they are faced with in schooling and society. Moving toward a critical visual praxis in our literacy teaching is essential for social justice and social change. This volume provides a powerful tool for teachers to use in the beautiful struggle ahead.

—Ebony Thomas, Assistant Professor of Reading, Writing, and Literacy, Graduate School of Education, University of Pennsylvania

Preface

This book could begin by regaling you with the dismal statistics in education today—low graduation rates, high disengagement, academic and economic disparities, and enough arguments about standards to make your hair curl—but we are all already too familiar with these figures and data bytes. We struggle to stay ahead of curricular, demographic, and societal changes in the microcosms that are our classrooms while awash in papers, meetings, and life commitments.

This book is not a silver bullet that addresses all of those demands, nor is it a book of ready-set lesson plans to roll out your next major unit. Instead it is a thoughtful approach that will help teachers understand the graphic novel, a format with great potential for engagement and learning, and use that format to meet the increasing demands of understanding disciplinary content and skills. While the book will not give you lesson plans, it will give you the tools you need to write them to suit the goals of your classroom and curriculum.

Stemming from our own personal interests in reading graphic novels, from our research in how students and teachers use them, and from our experiences as former high school teachers and current teacher educators, we want to share the potential of graphic novels as more than cute or gimmicky books that hook reluctant readers or books that dumb down content. We believe that graphic novels have vast potential to teach disciplinary content and habits of thinking and practice in truly powerful ways.

The graphic novel format has power in it. The close combination of image and text, so close that images and words must be read interdependently, has the capacity to carry so much context, humor, conceptual explanation, action, character development, mystery, and more, that it can be of great use in the classroom.

Graphic novels are sometimes touted as the texts to use with struggling or resistant readers. While, they *can* help engage this demographic, to view them only in this way undersells the complex and complicated ways that pictures and texts can work together to create meaning for readers. As Kim (2011) has written previously in regards to use of hip-hop in classrooms, using graphic novels is not just a new "condiment" to shake on the same old curriculum. Rather, it has the potential to transform curriculum both in content and structure in deep and meaningful ways.

Similarly, far from being a lowbrow, watered-down format that engages kids only because they can read the pictures and ignore the words, graphic novels have shown themselves to be a format that allows gifted creators to tell stories and explain concepts more fully than isolated text or film or video does. At the same time, the graphic novel format can help students learn to read traditional text, images, and the way text and image interact. In a world where most messages and narratives combine text and image, these are skills that students need.

Many scholars have written about the emerging demands of twenty-first-century literacies (Gee, 2014) and the increasingly multimodal ways in which we make meaning (Cope & Kalantzis, 2009) both with text and in the world. We must reimagine teaching and learning to embrace these expanded understandings of literacy and thinking and rise to meet these demands. The corresponding explosion of graphic novels that address disciplinary content and literacy skills offers a wealth of opportunity to address/converge some of these teaching demands. We hope that this book helps spark some ideas on how you can use graphic novels in your classrooms.

Like any book, this one came together with the help of many colleagues and friends, and the support of our families. In particular we would like to thank Tom Koerner and Carlie Wall at Rowman & Littlefield for their guidance and support; Ebony Elizabeth Thomas for writing a wonderful foreword; teachers who served as advance readers including Amy Boerman-Cornell, Jeff DeVries, and Kris Opie; and Dr. William Teale for his encouragement and brainstorming during an earlier iteration of this project.

Bill would also like to thank Trinity Christian College, where he teaches, for giving him a summer research grant, which gave him time to work on writing and editing the initial draft. Thanks as well to Ben Hatke, Marissa Moss, and Gary Schmidt, whose conversations about young adult literature and images were helpful. He would also thank his cowriters, his amazing students, his colleagues at Trinity and beyond, and his superlative wife and daughters for bringing so many good books to his attention and for their patience and good humor.

Jung would like to thank her fellow cowriters, Bill and Mike, for seeing this project to fruition after many years of talking about it. She thanks all of her students, past, present, and future, who have shared about their own experiences with graphic novels in the classrooms and keep her updated on new and exciting titles. Finally, she thanks her husband who still jokingly asks if the constant flood of new books is going to be "paid for" by her job, and her children, who are learning to read among this flood.

Michael would like to thank his colleagues at Northern Illinois University, especially Jerry Johns, Laurie Elish-Piper, Susan L'Allier, Corrine Wickens, and Donna Werderich who have apprenticed his writing. He thanks his students who have taught him more than he could have ever hoped to have taught them. Finally, Michael would like to thank his wife and daughters for their unwavering support and for encouraging his writing.

Graphic novels offer great potential for teachers and students to learn together. As a medium, graphic novels are still in a remarkable creative explosion of imaginative and wonderful new books. Teaching with them not only affords a host of opportunities for all learners, but they are fun to read and discuss. Enjoy the exploration into what graphic novels can do for your classroom.

Chapter One

Introduction

Can Graphic Novels Save the World?

As we write this introduction, refugees are seeking asylum in a Europe that doesn't seem to want them. Police officers have been accused of beating and killing African Americans in a cycle of fear and violence that sometimes has the officers in the sights of snipers. Undocumented immigrants in the United States suffer exploitation and bigotry. America's national politics seem ruled by obstructionism, extremism, and people talking past each other. News and information are increasingly difficult to verify and trust. Globally the nations of the world seem unable to stem the tide of global climate change. Human trafficking and income inequity make us wonder where justice is.

Given all these challenges that face our children, why are we writing a book about how to use overgrown comic books in the classroom? What can graphic novels offer a world plagued by inequity, injustice, and despair?

These are reasonable questions. However, we will argue that graphic novels are more than "overgrown comic books" and that, besides engaging readers and aiding in comprehension, graphic novels can be powerful tools to teach critical response to issues of inequity, injustice, mistrust, and despair. Such texts do not fulfill any of the functions mentioned earlier.

Sims Bishop (1990) describes how texts can function as windows (letting us see out into other cultures, experiences, and worlds), mirrors (showing us ourselves and how we fit into our context), and sliding glass doors (allowing us to step into other cultures and experiences). Many disciplinary texts in use in schools have been around for many years (sometimes decades) and reflect an older, middle-class, largely white worldview.

Graphic novels can open up new perspectives reflective to the cultures of some students while allowing other students to see cultures and perspectives

1

they may not be familiar with. Within the discussion, critical responses, challenges, responses, and engagement that follows, students can recognize injustice and brokenness, and consider ways to understand, improve, and challenge the world.

Before we get to how graphic novels can help your students learn to think critically and learn to make a difference in a broken world, however, we need to clear up a few misconceptions. To start with, graphic novels are more than overgrown comic books—they are a global phenomenon.

Whether in popular culture or in academic spheres, in the last few years, graphic novels (and/or comic books) have taken over. It seems almost every other major movie release is based on a graphic novel or comic book, and according to industry figures, children and adults alike are buying and reading graphic novels in greatly increasing numbers. After being labeled for almost seventy years as a lowbrow form meant to titillate and entertain, graphic novels have earned a new place in literature and society.

In 2015 alone, *This One Summer* by Jillian Tamaki and Mariko Tamaki, a story about two teenage girls trying to understand depression, boys, love, and life, won a Caldecott Honor Award; *El Deafo*, a biography of a young deaf girl navigating elementary school, won a Newbery Honor Award; *March: Book One*, a memoir of the civil rights era by Congressman John Lewis, won a Coretta Scott King Honor Award; and *Nimona* by Noelle Stevenson, the story of a girl who gets a job as an assistant to a supervillain and discovers he is more noble than she thought, was a National Book Award for Young People's Literature finalist.

In a single year, graphic novels won these four awards, arguably the most important in children's and young adult literature. They are standing on a foundation laid by award-winning graphic novels of the recent past including Gene Yang's *American Born Chinese* (a National Book Award finalist) and Art Spiegelman's *Maus* (which won the Pulitzer Prize). Such graphic novels are becoming more and more a staple of high school English classrooms.

Furthermore, within the context of globalization, graphic novels, often seen as an American invention, have become more respected worldwide as literature. While comic books were once banned in schools and even challenged as a negative influence in congressional hearings, graphic novels are now being taken more seriously by teachers, critics, and regular readers both as literature and art.

With major writers and artists including Neil Gaiman, Jane Yolen, Gene Yang, Alison Bechdel, Jeff Smith, Faith Hicks, George O'Connor, and others receiving international acclaim and recognition, graphic novels provide the potential for students to have greater exposure to a global understanding of the world. Recognizing this, educators have embraced the ability of graphic novels to engage students, and researchers have begun to undertake a closer examination of their value in classrooms. This book seeks to explore the real and unrealized potential of using graphic novels in secondary classrooms to teach both content *and* disciplinary thinking skills.

Sitting at the intersection of changing literacy practices, classrooms, and understandings of text and images, graphic novels adeptly use twenty-first-century skills. Maybe what contributed to this resurgence of interest in graphic novels is the changing nature of the way we understand and interact with different literacies. Less than a quarter of a century ago, most reading and writing was static, bound to the page, and often set apart from visual content. Educators, critics, and responsible adults often saw books that were heavily visual in content as the domain of children and readers who lacked the capacity to comprehend print-heavy texts.

In the age of the Internet and globalization, though, readers must continuously navigate texts that are inextricably bound with image. Whether navigating the World Wide Web or reposting the latest infographic or meme, competent readers need to be able to negotiate text, images, and sounds, as well as interpret the context of what they encounter. Text is no longer linear but requires fluidity in production, consumption, and interpretation.

The challenge of meeting the demands of reading these increasingly multimodal and complex texts hardly exists in a vacuum. Secondary teachers are expected to use increasingly challenging and authentic disciplinary texts to learn, communicate, and critique disciplinary knowledge in areas like history or science. Graphic novels are an excellent means of reaching those goals. Both challenging and authentic, graphic novels offer both format and content that can speak to the disciplinary demands required today.

In stark contrast to the solitary print-heavy textbook used in many classrooms, the range of texts valued in different disciplines and occupations is no longer limited to traditional printed texts. For example, historians draw upon a variety of primary source documents such as diaries, maps, and interviews to construct their understandings of an event. In fact, the graphic novel *Maus* is considered by many historians as an authentic historical account from the perspective of the son of a Holocaust survivor.

Students need support in reading a wide variety of texts in their disciplinary learning. Using graphic novels merely as a means of engaging students is insufficient. This fails to exploit fully the affordances of the graphic novel and sets students up for failure in meeting disciplinary demands. Graphic novels have an important place in the broad repertoire of classroom texts that provide students access to disciplinary knowledge construction—but they need the support of educators who can help them learn how to get the most from what graphic novels offer. This book will help teachers do that.

This book is primarily intended for grade 6–12 teachers and teacher candidates who wish to use graphic novels to reach disciplinary goals in the classroom. It can also help readers understand the variety of changes in teaching different literacies today, as well as provide a source of curricular and pedagogical ideas. However, because this book addresses the different demands of discipline-specific literacies, it can also help postsecondary instructors looking for a way to address these distinctions with their students.

Although we acknowledge the differences between disciplines, we chose not to separate the disciplines into distinct chapters. Instead, chapters highlight the specific skills, techniques, and affordances of graphic novels that are common to multiple disciplines. This underscores the disciplinary potential of graphic novels in a variety of contexts and also encourages interdisciplinary connections. For example, instead of reiterating how teachers can use a graphic novel like *Maus* for different disciplinary demands in multiple chapters, this book considers what such a graphic novel can offer overall and how different disciplines might use it for specific purposes.

In order to make navigating the book easier for the reader, we have arranged the chapters to follow an acronym (as former high school teachers and current literacy researchers we admit to a fondness for acronyms) and so this structure follows the word GRAPHIC. Specifically, GRAPHIC refers to:

Goals that graphic novels can help readers meet

Resources that can help meet those goals

Approaches that can focus learning (e.g., disciplinary thinking and practices, inquiry strategies)

Picture/text Hybridity: ways that images and text intersect and inform each other

Inquiry: tasks and strategies that support student curiosity and investigation using graphic novels

Critical response: ways to encourage students to critically respond to graphic novels through concluding assessments and culminating activities that acknowledge, celebrate, and assess the learning and work that students have done

While each chapter will focus on a particular element of this framework, some chapters may also use this structure to guide the reader through all the elements of building a strong graphic-novel-based unit.

This book, then, doesn't just look at engaging students with graphic novels, but truly explores how to use graphic novels to reach disciplinary teaching goals.

Chapter 2 provides an overview of disciplinary literacies and considers how disciplinary *goals* will help students learn new ways of thinking, questioning, and understanding.

Chapter 3 presents an overview of graphic novels, how to read them, what research has discovered about them, and how you can determine which graphic novel *resources* are most suitable for disciplinary teaching.

Chapter 4 looks at how graphic novels fit into disciplinary *approaches* for teaching science, technology, engineering, and mathematics.

Chapter 5 parallels chapter 4, but considers disciplinary approaches for using graphic novels in teaching the humanities. For the sake of our acronym, we'll just consider chapters 4 and 5 as together being about disciplinary approaches.

Chapter 6 considers some of the ways that *picture/text hybridity* affects the way students read and interpret graphic novels and how you can help students do that most effectively.

Chapter 7 gives an overview of how you can most effectively use graphic novels to teach *inquiry*-based approaches to your students.

Chapter 8 looks at ways to teach students to respond *critically* to graphic novel units. The chapter considers some approaches to assessment that allow students to do more than prove their knowledge by filling in bubble tests or summarizing their reading in book report forms.

Chapter 9 considers how graphic novels can help with interdisciplinary teaching (and looks at each part of the GRAPHIC acronym again).

And finally, chapter 10 draws some conclusions from our discussions. At the end of the book, you will see additional sections with annotated recommendations of graphic novels by discipline and age, as well as a list of online resources that will help you keep up with new graphic novels as they come out.

So if you have tried using graphic novels in the classroom already, or if you have been wanting to for some time, or if you are just considering the possibilities, get ready to explore the ways that graphic novels can do more in your classroom than just get your students' attention. They can help you teach your students to see each discipline—language arts, science, social studies, math, physical education, and others—as representing different ways of thinking and solving problems.

And in the world we live in, we are in desperate need of new perspectives, ways of seeing, and solutions. If graphic novels can help us do that, they may really help save the world—not by donning a cape and a mask and fighting aliens or supervillains, but by providing material for students to read, comprehend, think critically, and respond by tackling injustice and inequity in our world.

Chapter Two

The Role of Disciplinary Literacy for Teaching with Graphic Novels

If you are reading this book, it is likely you are a teacher, and there is a good chance you are also an excellent reader. Even the best readers, however, while in middle school and high school, struggled with the reading assignments in one or two subjects.

Maybe reading history came easy to you, but it seemed impossible to determine what the poems in English class were supposed to be saying. Maybe reading novels was enjoyable, but you found the charts and graphs in science textbooks utterly incomprehensible. Maybe the math textbook was easy to understand completely, but the physical education test on the rules of volleyball was impossibly difficult. Even teachers who consider themselves great readers may wonder, "Why are reading assignments in my favorite subject easy and enjoyable, while reading assignments in my least favorite subject feel like they are written in an alien language?"

One challenge is that different academic subjects not only teach different content, but they teach it in different ways. Researchers have known for a long time that there is a strong connection between content area learning and improving students' literacy (Gray, 1925; Herber, 1970). In spite of that, approaches to content area instruction in secondary (grades 6–12) contexts rarely focus on literacy instruction. Explicit content area literacy instruction usually gets pushed aside in favor of topical content instruction (O'Brien, Stewart, & Moje, 1995).

Content area teachers may feel that literacy instruction is not their responsibility and that instruction should focus on content. Despite this resistance, in order to teach students how to comprehend the textbook in a given discipline, teachers have found that several content area literacy strategies are useful and effective.

Examples of cognitive literacy strategies include activating prior knowledge, clarifying, making predictions, or summarizing. These strategic behav-
iors are embedded into content area literacy strategies such as GIST, possible
sentences, QARs, and semantic mapping, which assume that approaches to
reading can be applied universally regardless of whether the student is reading a mathematics text or a primary source in history class.

Cognitive strategy instruction in the form of such content area literacy
strategies also has limitations, however. Although teachers have found cognitive strategy instruction to be effective for teaching traditional print texts,
such instruction is less commonly used for the range of multimodal texts
used for content area learning. Additionally, cognitive strategy instruction
assumes a more generalized approach to reading and does not take into
account textual and discourse differences in the various content areas. Disciplinary literacy instruction is an approach that puts disciplinary learning in
the foreground by focusing on language and text demands.

DISCIPLINARY LITERACY: WHAT IS IT?

Disciplinary literacy is an approach to improving the literacy of adolescents
learning to read expository texts within specific school subjects (math, language arts, history, science, etc.) by focusing on the ways of reading and
understanding that are unique to each discipline. The premise of disciplinary
literacy is that a learner needs to understand how texts and talk are created
and used in a discipline in order to fully participate in the discipline. Some
researchers have thus defined disciplinary literacy in this way:

> Disciplinary literacy involves the use of reading, reasoning, investigating,
> speaking, and writing required to learn and form complex content knowledge
> appropriate to a particular discipline. (McConachie & Petrosky, 2010, p. 16)

An apprenticeship model of instruction can support students' reading,
writing, thinking, and communicating in the disciplines (Schoenbach, Greenleaf, & Murphy, 2012). That is, teachers design learning environments that
make use of developmentally appropriate activities that help students learn
disciplinary practices.

To scaffold adolescents' skill and agency in constructing knowledge,
teachers can encourage disciplinary inquiry through activities like document-
based questions (DBQs) in history, science labs or experiments in science,
and critical analysis essays with literature. However, these activities should
help students engage in disciplinary inquiry that apprentices cognitive skills
(i.e., thinking like a historian, scientist, or literary critic) with a range of
disciplinary texts and tools rather than laying out a prescribed path to a fixed
and predictable answer.

A disciplinary literacies approach also offers the promise of apprenticing students into the disciplinary communities that use these specific cognitive skills and knowledge of linguistic markers. But perhaps more importantly, such an approach opens up opportunities for students to gain access to the ways knowledge is constructed and communicated.

Disciplinary literacy instruction gives students the thinking and language necessary to critique content and the confidence necessary to construct knowledge for their own purposes. This allows young people to build the capacities necessary to be able to construct instead of simply consume knowledge. Disciplinary literacies are fundamentally about knowledge building instead of knowledge banking and making students into participants in the discourse of different literacies instead of only passive rote learners.

To apprentice students into disciplinary literacies, there are core elements that students must understand. First, disciplinary literacies are predicated on the beliefs and common understanding that undergird thinking and doing in that discipline. These *ways of knowing* in a discipline shape how one approaches learning. For example, literary critics and accomplished readers approach literature as a window into the human experience, while historians view the past as approximated and contested, and scientists see a constantly expanding world where theories are challenged and tested (Goldman et al., 2016). *Ways of knowing* are critical to help students understand how texts are used in their respective disciplines.

In addition to apprenticing *ways of knowing* in the discipline, designing activities that encourage *habits of thinking* that experts in the disciplines employ is critical. Disciplinary *habits of thinking* refer to the types of cognitive processes used when making meaning with a disciplinary text. Experts in different academic disciplines use distinct practices to understand what they read. For example, historians pay close attention to authorship and continuously compare different sources with one another (Wineburg, 1991). Scientists in the field of physics focus their attention on new information, especially that which contradicts what they have previously thought about the topic (Bazerman, 1985).

As such, explicit instruction around these types of *habits of thinking* are needed since they are not the typical ways the readers tend to approach text. In addition to the *habits of thinking*, learning activities that leverage the *habits of practice* valued in the disciplines are needed as well. *Habits of practice* include disciplinary *habits of thinking*, but they also incorporate how members of disciplinary communities talk, how they interact interpersonally or intertextually, and how they act when engaged in the discipline (Wickens, Manderino, Parker, & Jung, 2015).

These *habits of practice* can include constructing models, engaging in debate, persevering in problem solving, or collaboratively making meaning. *Habits of practice* widen disciplinary literacies from only thinking tasks but also what it means to be fully engaged in the discipline. The *ways of knowing, habits of thinking, and habits of practice* all get taken up through the texts that are used for disciplinary inquiry. Table 2.1 represents some of the ways these constructs make up disciplinary practice.

Disciplinary literacies are predicated on learning through text and talk. By taking this approach, this book moves from reading textbooks and traditional expositions of disciplinary content to the multiple types of texts that students can use to communicate, construct, and critique disciplinary knowledge.

Table 2.1.   Examples of Disciplinary Literacies

Discipline	Ways of Knowing	Habits of Thinking	Habits of Practice	Texts
English Language Arts	Literature and literary nonfiction can serve as a window and mirror for human experiences.	Demonstrating a critical stance Interpreting Responding	Reading for literary devices Interrogating the reliability of a narrator Examining symbolism in literature	Literature Poems Essays Lyrics
History	The past is contested and approximated. Historical events are interpreted from a range of perspectives.	Sourcing Contextualization Corroboration Reconstructing the past	Reconciling competing accounts of the past Identifying causal relationships	Primary sources Secondary sources Textbooks Maps Photographs
Math	Math uses proofs to find truth and identify errors in logic or computation.	Justifying Solving Proving	Quantitative reasoning Communicating with precision Persevering in problem solving	Textbooks Problem sets Graphs
Science	Science is a constantly expanding field where constructs and theories are challenged and tested.	Questioning Hypothesizing Model building	Constructing models of scientific processes Writing scientific explanations Reading nonlinguistic, scientific representations	Three-dimensional models Data tables Graphs Scientific explanations

Photographs, podcasts, videos, digitized media, and so on, are all ways that different disciplines represent knowledge.

Because this is a book about graphic novels, our focus on disciplinary literacies considers how readers use the elements of graphic novels to make meaning. Graphic novels can serve as excellent disciplinary texts and allow students to learn to both communicate with and critique disciplinary knowledge.

WHY DISCIPLINARY LITERACIES AND GRAPHIC NOVELS?

Given the range of textual representations used in the disciplines, why dedicate an entire book to one form: the graphic novel? Frequently thought of as supplemental in disciplinary learning, graphic novels offer affordances that are crucial to effective teaching in many disciplines. For example, in English language arts, teachers know that if students can view a live Shakespearean production or see the latest film adaptation of a classic novel, they will have an easier time visualizing the action. Visualization is a key component of the comprehension, analysis, and critical interpretation of literature and literary nonfiction.

In addition, visual representations of scientific models are critical to understanding complex explanations of scientific phenomena such as the water cycle or the circulatory system. Historical accounts such as political cartoons, photographs, and maps are essential to generating a more complete account of the past. Unfortunately in classrooms, disciplinary texts are too often represented only as print sources, decontextualized from the broader everyday skills of meaning making that we employ whenever we look at a wide variety of texts that mediate our lived experiences.

Graphic novels are one such example of a multimodal text that can be used to deepen disciplinary understanding. Graphic novels offer affordances that capitalize on both visual and written representation as well as chances to interrogate texts from a disciplinary standpoint. For example, a historical graphic novel such as *Safe Area Gorazde* embeds primary and secondary source material, maps, and first-person accounts of the Bosnian War. The text also provides opportunities for students to critically examine the accounts presented, the author's choice of visual representations, and the overall argument made about the effects of the Bosnian War.

One approach to help build that capacity is to teach authentic inquiry rather than convergent questioning that seeks a single correct answer. Teachers can scaffold and support inquiry practices but should seek to release responsibility to their students so they can ask and seek meaning to their own disciplinary questions. While that may seem lofty, it is the best way to support student learning while also valuing their interests and cultural knowledge.

Disciplinary literacy instruction then draws on the habits of thinking to interrogate the texts that are central in the disciplines. Students learn to construct disciplinary texts using norms, conventions, genres, and linguistic patterns that have evolved in the discipline. Teaching isolated sets of disciplinary skills is insufficient because the disciplines are not static. They are historical, contextual, and contested sites of organized bodies of knowledge. Therefore, students need to be apprenticed into disciplinary inquiry.

While some might argue that a disciplinary literacy approach may only reinforce the separation of the disciplines, we would respond that disciplinary literacy is a basic commitment to the tentative and contested nature of knowledge through apprenticed inquiry that can empower youth to critically engage with their world. The use of literacies is critical to develop habits of thinking, cultural tools, habits of practice, and ways of knowing.

Our young people deserve opportunities to read and write the word and the world as contributing and critical citizens. Graphic novels provide opportunities to approximate disciplinary inquiry using texts that facilitate agency for students. Disciplinary literacies are fundamentally about knowledge building instead of knowledge banking.

GRAPHIC NOVELS FOR DISCIPLINARY LEARNING

So how can a teacher plan to use graphic novels to enhance instruction in the academic disciplines? The GRAPHIC format outlined in the first chapter aligns well to the lesson or unit planning process (see figure 2.1).

Goals that graphic novels can help readers meet

Resources that can help meet those goals

Approaches that can focus learning (e.g., disciplinary thinking and practices, inquiry strategies)

Picture/text **H**ybridity: ways that images and text intersect and inform each other

Inquiry: tasks and strategies that support student inquiry, comprehension, and understanding

Critical response: What are the opportunities students have to critically interrogate the text and its ideas?

The GRAPHIC framework is a recursive process rather than a linear set of steps to follow in order. GRAPHIC employs solid pedagogical design principles for disciplinary learning but with a specific focus on the use of graphic novels.

Figure 2.1.   The GRAPHIC Framework

Initially, teachers should set disciplinary literacy goals for instruction. In selecting disciplinary learning outcomes, consider the affordances that graphic novels provide in meeting those goals. For example, if a teacher wants students to be able to examine the ways that authors use characterization to establish a narrative, then a graphic novel like Gene Yang's *American Born Chinese* can provide ample opportunities. Students can investigate the author's use of characterization both in the written prose but also in the visual representation of the different identities that the book uses to reflect various aspects of a single person (apparently). In a traditional novel, the irony in the caricatured portrayal of Chin-kee might pass over students' heads. But if the teacher encourages students to consider visual portrayal, Chin-kee's exaggerated buck teeth, skin color, and clothing (which looks like it came straight from a Fu Manchu movie) make it easier for student-readers to detect the sarcasm and irony.

Next, consider the wealth of graphic novel resources that fit those specific disciplinary literacy goals. These may be excerpts of a graphic novel, a complete graphic novel, or excerpts from multiple graphic novels. Examples of useful graphic novels are embedded in each chapter of this book. Chapter

10 includes some additional lists for particular disciplines and suggests some resources to find more.

Once the texts are selected, decide on approaches to support disciplinary learning. In order to teach with graphic novels, teachers must consider the picture/text hybridity. That is how the words and images converge or are juxtaposed to create meaning for the reader. Just as readers need strategies to make meaning from printed text, readers also need strategies to make sense of visual texts. Analysis of the picture/text hybridity can help determine the instruction supports to be used with the graphic novel. Finally, provide opportunities for students to critically respond to the graphic novel in a variety of ways. Table 2.2 is a sample planning guide using the GRAPHIC framework in a history class.

Table 2.1 demonstrates how to engage deeply with the text in a way that develops disciplinary learning. The use of graphic novels has great potential to deepen students' disciplinary literacy skills. The goal of disciplinary litera-

Table 2.2.   Example GRAPHIC Planning Sheet for History

Class: U.S. History
Unit: Civil Rights Movement

Goals	Students will be able to source, contextualize, and corroborate sources to construct an interpretation of why the civil rights movement was successful.
Resources	Textbook, primary accounts, *Eyes on the Prize* documentary, *March I and II*
Approaches	Because the civil rights movement is complex, I want to start with some questions. Because the past is not fixed but rather full of various interpretations, I want students to recognize points of view. Therefore I will start the unit with *March I* to engage my students from a particular perspective. Then we will look at other perspectives through *Eyes on the Prize* and primary accounts such as Malcolm X, Melba Pattillo Beals, and Angela Davis. After investigating these multiple accounts we will return to *March II* and look specifically at the Selma march.
Picture/Text Hybridity	In *March I* and *II* it will be important for readers to recognize how John Lewis is narrating the past from the present and through the lens of his preparing to attend President Barack Obama's inauguration in 2008.
Inquiry	We will begin with a casual inquiry question, *Why was the civil rights movement successful?* To spark the inquiry, we will read *March I.* Throughout the inquiry we will use *March I* and *II* and compare and contrast with other sources to investigate the inquiry question.
Critical Response	Throughout the unit, students will be asked to critically interrogate John Lewis's accounts based on his position in the movement. At the end of the inquiry, students will create their own response to the question, *Why was the civil rights movement successful?*

cies is not to create mini-historians, scientists, or literary critics but to give student-readers the chance to learn new ways of thinking, comprehending, problem solving, and constructing knowledge.

Disciplinary literacies approximate the reading and writing practices of insiders so that students know how the texts they are reading are produced, the many ways that experts communicate knowledge, the standards for legitimacy accepted in the discipline, and ultimately the ways to construct knowledge about disciplinary topics.

Chapter Three

What Are Graphic Novels?

How Do They Work? Why Would Teachers Want to Use Them, Anyway? What Is the Best Way to Teach with Them?

Brian Selznick's *The Invention of Hugo Cabret* looks like a thick novel from the outside, but when you open the pages, you discover a story told by page after page of penciled drawings, with occasional regular text for several pages, then back to the drawings. Is this a graphic novel or just a novel with pictures?

The Arrival by Shaun Tan is laid out like a comic book, with multiple panels per page telling the story of an immigrant coming to a new country. However, there is no readable text in the entire book, only illegible symbols from time to time conveying that the main character cannot understand the language of the new country he has arrived in. The book looks like a picture book for kids just learning to read, but is often used in middle school and high school. Is it a graphic novel or a picture book for older kids?

John Lewis, Andrew Aydin, and Nate Powell's *March: Books One, Two, and Three* is Lewis's autobiographical description of his involvement with the civil rights movement. The story is told in a comic book format but is nonfiction. Can this be a graphic novel if it isn't a novel?

Ms. Marvel: No Normal is a collaboration between writer G. Willow Wilson and artist Adrian Alphona. Though it is bound as a softcover book, it contains issues 1 through 5 of the regular run comic book *Ms. Marvel*. The story concerns a teenage Muslim girl named Kamala Khan who finds she has amazing powers and must reconcile her dreams with the concerns of her parents, friends, and brother. Is this a graphic novel or a collection of comic books?

Gene Yang's *Boxers* and *Saints* uses two books to tell the stories of two people caught up in China's Boxer Rebellion. Yang uses the tricks and tools of the comic book world—panels, speech balloons, thought bubbles, narration boxes, and so on—to tell a fictional story set in an important historical period. Of all the examples listed here, Yang's work perhaps most closely fits the traditional definition of a graphic novel.

The term "graphic novel" is a misnomer in more than one way. Graphic novels are neither exclusively graphic, nor are they exclusively novels. Other, more descriptive terms have been proposed, including Will Eisner's term "sequential art," but the term that seems to have stuck is the term "graphic novel." Put simply, a graphic novel is any book-length narrative that uses the conventions (or symbolic language) of a comic book to tell a story. Comic books use all sorts of conventions that readers come to understand, including word balloons, narration boxes, panel divisions to define scenes, and so on.

Some graphic novel creators prefer the generic term "comics," but this term doesn't distinguish between newspaper comic strips, thirty-page comic books featuring superheroes, and book-length graphic novels.

A graphic novel, like a comic book, uses words and images to tell a story or relate information. If the words and images never appear in the same panel, what you are looking at is probably not a graphic novel. Graphic novels can include fiction, memoir, biography, self-help books, collections of short stories, adaptations of classic literature, surveys of history, and primary source documents.

Of the examples listed above, *March: Book One, Two*, and *Three* and *Boxers* and *Saints* most clearly fit our definition. This definition would include Art Spiegelman's *Maus* (a fictionalized memoir); Marjane Satrapi's *Persepolis* (also a memoir, but not fictionalized); Jim Ottaviani and Maris Wicks's *Primates: The Fearless Science of Jane Goodall, Dian Fossey, and Birute Galdikas* (three connected biographies); Mat Johnson and Warren Pleece's *Incognegro* (a historical novel based in part on real events); and Katherine Arnoldi's *The Amazing True Story of a Teenage Single Mom* (a memoir meant to make a particular point).

Brian Selznick's *The Invention of Hugo Cabret* and *The Arrival* by Shaun Tan fall within the larger heading of graphica, which refers to any book that combines images and words. Since these two books only use one or two elements of the symbolic language employed by comic books (and do not combine text and image within panels), they do not primarily depend upon the direct interaction of images and text, and do not have the full range of affordances discussed earlier. Though such texts can certainly be useful in the classroom, this discussion will focus on graphic novels that more closely fit the definition (and as such prove to be better examples and illustrations).

Some teachers, librarians, artists, and parents occasionally suggest that a graphic novel is really just an overgrown comic book with pretensions. There are, however, important differences between the comic book format and that of the graphic novel. Certainly both formats can have well-written stories and stories that are not so well written, excellent art and art that is unimaginative or disconnected. Certainly both are told with similar symbolic conventions. Yet the two formats yield different affordances and constraints.

The real distinguishing feature of graphic novels is their length. Comic books usually run between twenty-one and thirty-two pages, not including advertising. That length determines to some extent what sort of story can be told. Graphic novels have no particular page limit, which gives them more freedom to tell whatever length story they want and usually allows them to explore their subjects with greater depth (consider the difference between the sort of story one can tell in a half-hour television show versus what story can be told in a feature-length movie).

To be fair, some well-known and critically acclaimed graphic novels (e.g., Alan Moore's *Watchmen* or Neil Gaiman's *Sandman* series) began in serialized comic book form, but their creators envisioned them as a single continuous body of work. *Ms. Marvel: No Normal* is technically a graphic novel, but this book will go into depth about bound collections of comic books. The episodic nature of such work makes it more difficult to use with students unfamiliar with the graphic novel format and all the intertextual connections within the comic book world.

So while the term "graphic novel" encompasses a remarkable range of fiction, nonfiction, and memoir using a variety of styles to reach many different audiences, there are some books that are sometimes called graphic novels which fit better into the broader term of graphica.

GRAPHIC NOVELS AND MANGA

So then, what is the difference between graphic novels and manga? Think of it this way: even as all graphic novels are graphica, but not all graphica are graphic novels; in the same way, all manga are graphic novels, but not all graphic novels are manga.

Manga refers to a style of art made popular in Japan that has since been picked up in other countries in Asia and eventually the United States. Characterists of manga style include characters with disproportionately big eyes (often, but not always), backgrounds that are often more suggested, blurred, or impressionistic than photorealistic, and some distinctive symbolic elements (e.g., drawing an adult character as a little kid when depicting childish emotions).

The term "manga" also refers to a particular format of graphic novel—usually paperback, black-and-white art that extends to the edges of the pages and usually reads from right to left. Manga are bound and usually explore a longer story line (which casts them as graphic novels) but are also sometimes serialized and have open-ended, inconclusive story lines like comic books. There are many subgenres of manga.

Sometimes people confuse the terms "anime" and "manga." Anime refers to animated movies done in the manga style, but the term "manga" refers only to printed graphic novels.

There is a similar confusion between the terms "cartoons" and "comics." Cartoon usually refers to an animated television show (*Scooby Doo*, *SpongeBob SquarePants*, and *The Simpsons* are all examples). The term "comic strip" usually refers to one-panel to eight-panel comic strips that appear in the newspaper. The term "comic" usually refers to comic books (thirty- to forty-page, stapled periodic booklets sold in comic book stores that usually feature superheroes or funny animals).

So, with the definition of graphic novels and comics clear, the next questions one might ask is, are these things at all useful in the classroom? Has research discovered anything about how graphic novels might best be used for teaching?

A BRIEF HISTORY OF COMICS AND GRAPHIC NOVELS AND EDUCATIONAL RESEARCH

It is hard to identify when comic books first came about. Some people argue that early medieval tapestries and cave paintings use some of the same techniques as comic books. Most experts agree that comic books really came into their own in the 1930s in the United States. They made the transition from newspaper inserts to stand-alone comic books and once Superman and Batman came along, comics achieved an all-time popularity level.

Early educational research on comic books in the forties and fifties tended to concentrate on the words only. The images were seen at best as neutral, and at worst, as a distraction. Despite this, researchers like Paul Witty (1941; Witty & Sizemore, 1955) saw potential in comic books to fight illiteracy. Other researchers in that time investigated student interest in comic books and the relationship between comic books and grades—discovering that students who read comic books correlated with higher scores on the Stanford Achievement tests (Heisler, 1948).

In 1954, a psychologist named Frederick Wertham published a book called *Seduction of the Innocent* that argued that graphic novels caused juvenile delinquency. Although his research methods were wholly discredited in later years, his book soon got the attention of presidential hopeful Senator

Estes Kefauver, who held hearings on Wertham's book, resulting in a huge decline of interest in comic books. As comic book readership declined, so did research into comics' educational value.

In the 1970s, researchers began once again to consider the possible educational value of comic books. Researchers like Arlin and Roth (1978) showed a correlation between comic book reading and initial positive attitudes toward reading, while Swain (1978) correlated high academic achievement with comic book reading.

When Art Spiegelman's *Maus* won a Pulitzer Prize in 1992, researchers began to shift their focus from comic books to graphic novels. Though there were two or three studies done in the 1990s, graphic novel research really began to take off as the new millennium began.

Many of the new graphic novel studies were qualitative, trying to figure out what the research questions should be, as opposed to the comic book research that was usually quantitative—attempting to measure whatever could be measured. There were also many articles that put forth ideas and theories but were not tied to any actual research, making it difficult to determine how seriously to take them. More recently, however, graphic novel researchers have begun conducting studies that can answer some specific questions about graphic novels in the classroom.

DO STUDENT READERS EVEN LIKE GRAPHIC NOVELS?

Many do. Some don't. In his 2004 book *The Power of Reading: Insights from the Research*, Stephen Krashen argues passionately for the value of letting students read books that they find engaging and includes graphic novels in his list of high-interest options for student-readers. However, it would be a mistake to assume that absolutely all readers are attracted to graphic novels.

In 2006, Sean Cavazos-Kottke tracked five gifted and talented middle school students during a browsing session in a bookstore and then interviewed them about their choices, interests, and motivations. The study found that choices varied from student to student, but that one student in particular was interested in graphic novels.

That same year, Joel Warrican conducted a similar study in a high school in the Caribbean. Warrican brought into his classroom a wide variety of high-interest reading materials into his classroom, including magazines, high-interest biographies, and graphic novels. His seventeen students, all identified as lower-track readers, then recorded their time spent reading each day.

Warrican saw no significant change in reading times after the high-interest materials were brought into his classroom. In interviewing the students about particular materials, he found that his students had never read a graphic novel before, thought they were mostly for children, and had been disappointed to find that they contained so many words.

So from the start, research indicated that different types of readers (gifted readers and struggling readers), in different places (the United States and the West Indies) with different levels of experience reading graphic novels, will react to them differently.

Other studies began to find out with more detail which sorts of students were interested in graphic novels and which weren't. Hughes-Hassell and Rodge (2007) surveyed 584 urban minority students and found that 44 percent were interested in reading comic books or graphic novels. In 2008, Robin Moeller conducted focus groups with high school students to determine whether female readers thought of graphic novels as "boy books." She found that females did not think this—though she also found that boys found reading graphic novels more rewarding than girls did.

Clare Snowball (2008) conducted focus groups with forty-one teenagers and asked them about reading and libraries. Snowball found that the appeal of graphic novels was not universal, and, in fact, was polarized with some students enthusiastically enamored of graphic novels, and others scathingly dismissive.

Interestingly, the studies of student interest up to this point were mostly looking at student interest in the context of leisure reading—in which the young reader might be expected to have predetermined preferences. Ask a student what he or she prefers to read and the usual answer will be a single genre: science fiction, sports books, romance, mystery, and so on. It is often in the context of school that we are introduced to new texts, new genres, and new formats. Because the term "graphic novel" refers to a format (a way of presenting a story) rather than a genre (a particular type of story), graphic novels may be a good way to get students to cross genres.

Research over the next few years confirmed that both students and teachers valued graphic novels, but also revealed shortcomings in knowledge about how to use them for instruction. In 2010, David Seelow surveyed and interviewed a group of 160 college students in six classes over a three-year period. The college students were all enrolled in Seelow's Introduction to Literature course in a technical college that specializes in programs in math, science, and engineering.

Seelow's class used several texts as instructional materials, including one graphic novel, which they could choose (ranging from Neil Gaiman's *Sandman* to Art Spiegelman's *Maus*). At the end of the semester, an average of 94 percent of the students chose the graphic novel as their favorite text.

In a doctoral dissertation, Stefanie Droste (2012) engaged in an experimental study that divided students into two treatment groups to determine whether students can become as deeply emotionally involved with graphic novels as they can with conventional reading. Her results showed that readers seem equally likely to become emotionally involved with graphic novels.

Research has shown that many teachers have interest in graphic novels as well. In 2009, Callahan interviewed and surveyed eleven middle school and high school teachers and found that though they had a positive view of graphic novels, they did not use them as teaching tools. Lapp, Wolsey, Fisher, and Frey (2011–2012) surveyed sixty teachers about using graphic novels in the classroom and found that "though the teachers reported willingness to use graphic novels [in the classroom] . . . they are limited in their attempts to do so by lack of instructional models, lack of graphic novels in the classroom, and their own level of comfort with the [format]" (p. 23).

And so overall we conclude that many school-aged readers (and teachers) like the graphic novel format, though some other students don't. The research seems to imply that one factor influencing the popularity of graphic novels may be familiarity with the format, though additional research needs to be done in this area.

The research also indicates that most young readers encounter graphic novels in the context of their leisure reading rather than in the context of required school reading. It is clear that teachers appreciate graphic novels and are open to using the format but are uncertain of how to do so. There is also some evidence that graphic novel readers can enter into that reading as deeply as conventional readers do.

ARE GRAPHIC NOVELS GOOD FOR LEARNING?

The answer, according to the research, is yes, but it is complicated. The answer depends on what kind of learning and what kind of graphic novel we are talking about. Graphic novel research is still relatively young, and so it can only answer this question partially.

Most studies looking at this question focus on classroom practice. Frey and Fisher, in 2004, conducted one of the earliest studies that looked at this question. They focused on the research writing skills of thirty-two ninth graders identified as struggling readers and writers. Fisher and Frey found that graphic novels seemed to help with student engagement and discussion. In a culminating project, their students created their own graphic novels, and Fisher and Frey argued that the project helped improve writing skills.

Sean Connors (2012) also looked at graphic novels and reading skills. He surveyed and observed six high school students as they read and discussed four graphic novels and found that "when readers possess the background knowledge needed to approximate the role of the implied reader—that is, the imaginary audience for whom authors envision themselves writing—they are capable of engaging with graphic novels in ways that readers who lack experience with the form, or who question its literary merit, are not."

Leckbee (2005) and Doran (2008) both reported on anecdotal evidence of classroom practice involving graphic novels. Leckbee describes how the image and text work together to allow students to easily become immersed in the world the graphic novel portrays. Doran describes how the format of graphic novels can help students look at stories in ways that allow them to be more critical and thoughtful.

Sylvia Pantaleo (2011) examined one seventh grader's learning in the context of a classroom project using four graphic novels. Pantaleo reported that her study revealed "how Stefina's participation and engagement in a particular classroom community of practice affected her learning of the content and concepts under study" (p. 39).

Other studies consider the value that graphic novels might hold as classroom resources. In 2010, Michael Boatright conducted a content analysis of several graphic novels that depicted immigrant experiences and speculated that such stories could be helpful for students to engage the complexity of immigration issues. Heidi Hammond (2009) looked at how twenty-three high school seniors read the graphic novel *American Born Chinese* and determined that "graphic novels are capable of presenting serious issues and students felt they should be included in the school curriculum" (p. 30).

CAN GRAPHIC NOVELS HELP ENGLISH LANGUAGE LEARNERS IMPROVE IN READING COMPREHENSION?

Here again, the answer seems to be yes, but looking at the research can help create a clearer idea of how graphic novels can make a difference. Bridges (2009) and Monnin (2009) reported anecdotal evidence that graphic novels help struggling English language learners (ELLs) in specific classroom contexts. In 2009, Christian Chun conducted a case study of one high school student. His analysis led him to argue that graphic novels in the secondary school classroom help develop critical literacies of English language learners. He further found that graphic novels increased the student's engagement in reading and also encouraged social interaction.

Jessica Chang (2011) analyzed class blog posts and conducted a focus group with five ELL students and five non-ELL students and found that responses to social justice issues were similar in both groups. All of these studies seem to indicate that graphic novels have a lot to offer an ELL class.

Martinez-Roldan and Newcomer (2011) examined how two students who were recent immigrants responded to the wordless picture book *The Arrival* by Shaun Tan. The study found that students from different cultures, ethnicities, and backgrounds were able to use what happens between the panels to understand the broader narrative. The study revealed a sophisticated interpretive activity that can offer teachers insights into what their immigrant students can do as readers.

All of this research seems favorable to the conclusion that graphic novels can support ELL students. However, it is worth noting that Amy Baker (2011) engaged in a research review and her analysis indicated that while graphic novels can help many struggling ELLs, the effect may not be universal.

DO GRAPHIC NOVELS PROMOTE CRITICAL THINKING, MEDIA LITERACY, MULTIMODAL UNDERSTANDING, AND OTHER NEW WAYS OF READING THE WORLD?

Apparently, yes. People often associate the format of graphic novels—the frames and pictures and word bubbles—with children's comic books about Donald Duck and Mickey Mouse, with comic strips like *Peanuts*, *Calvin and Hobbes*, *Boondocks*, and *Zits*, and with adolescent comic heroes like Superman and Spider-Man. This makes it easy to dismiss graphic novels, which use the same format, as somehow of lesser quality, as containing shallower content, and as requiring less skill to make sense of.

Researchers speak of how any format—regular text novels, movies, PowerPoint presentations, and so forth—have affordances and constraints. Affordances are the ways that format allows creators to reach their audience effectively. So regular novels allow us to see inside the minds of the characters. Movies can not only show the action, but influence our emotions with soundtracks. PowerPoint presentations can use images and visual cues to hold the audience's attention, and so on.

Constraints, on the other hand, are ways in which formats limit creators. Regular text novels usually do not include pictures, and so the writer has to convey visuals through description. Movies can only show characters' emotions through facial expressions or occasional voice-overs and cannot tell the audience directly what the character is feeling. PowerPoint presentations are limited in how many words can fit on a slide and still be legible.

Research has shown, however, that not only do graphic novels offer a rigorous interpretive challenge, but further, they offer affordances that are useful in any academic discipline, including critical thinking, media literacy, multimodal understanding, and other new interpretive approaches for students to learn.

In 2006, Gretchen Schwartz analyzed five graphic novels and determined that graphic novels "offer teachers the opportunity to implement critical media literacy in the classroom—literacy that affirms diversity, gives voice to all, and helps students examine ideas and practices that promulgate inequity" (pp. 61–62). In 2008, Katie Monnin engaged in a case study of a teacher and a twelve-year-old student and found that both the student and the teacher read the images and words in the graphic novel *Bone* on multiple levels, including as readers for school and readers for self.

In 2011, Stergios Botzakis looked at twelve adults who frequented a comic book store. He asked them about ways in which reading graphic novels had influenced their lives. He wrote about one participant, whom Botzakis called Roger, who described his reading practices as having "critical, moral, literary, and dialogic dimensions" (p. 113). In fact, it may be that the pop culture aspect of the graphic novel format makes it less intimidating and easier for students to approach critically.

So while the research is not particularly broad in this area, evidence suggests that graphic novels have affordances for helping students engage in higher-order thinking practices.

ARE GRAPHIC NOVELS EFFECTIVE IN ENGAGING RELUCTANT OR STRUGGLING READERS?

It depends. Early research into this question assumed that since graphic novels feature images as well as words, that the images would scaffold learning for reluctant or struggling readers. As researchers continue to learn more about how readers comprehend graphic novels, they are discovering that graphic novel reading requires strong visual interpretive skills as well as the ability to comprehend traditional text.

Phillip Crawford (2009) and Gomes and Carter (2010) assert that graphic novels are a good way of engaging reluctant readers. Gavigan (2011) conducted a graphic novel book club and did attitudinal surveys before and after the club. Survey results suggested that all four subjects indicated an increase in how they valued reading after the graphic novel book club intervention. Hughes, King, Perkins, and Fuke (2011) did case studies of two different graphic-novel-based literature programs implemented in instructing twelve- to fifteen-year-olds. Hughes et al. argued that reading graphic novels "can be used to engage reluctant students while developing the multimodal literacy skills needed for success in the 21st century" (p. 610).

In 2007, April Lamanno looked at fourteen special education students from ages fifteen to nineteen and found that graphic novels did not improve their reading skills or motivation. Part of the reason this finding is so contradictory to the studies cited earlier may be that the subjects in Lamanno's study were instructed in CORI (concept-oriented reading instruction) and generic content area methods, but not in how to read a graphic novel. Though graphic novels may ultimately prove effective for engaging struggling readers, at minimum, some sort of orientation to eye movement through panel layouts, how to read speech balloons in order, and other aspects of the unique language of the graphic novel format is necessary for the success of the struggling reader.

ARE GRAPHIC NOVELS EFFECTIVE IN TEACHING DEAF STUDENTS?

There are only two studies that look at this question, but the answer seems to be yes. Smetana, Odelson, Burns, and Grisham (2009) analyzed graphic novels that were targeted for high school students and found that they had particular affordances for teaching deaf students. Britt White (2011) also offered anecdotal support that graphic novels help increase reading comprehension in students with hearing loss.

ARE GRAPHIC NOVELS USEFUL IN TEACHING DIFFERENT ACADEMIC DISCIPLINES?

Of course, like conventional books, individual graphic novels vary greatly in usefulness for the disciplinary classroom. The question here is really whether the graphic novel format offers any unique affordances for the study of each academic discipline. The answer to this question lies in the research on the affordances of graphic novels for each academic discipline. This includes research about English, history, math, and science, though unfortunately there is no research as of this writing on the use of graphic novels for the fine arts, physical education, or other disciplines.

HOW CAN GRAPHIC NOVELS BE USED TO TEACH ENGLISH?

Some studies approaching this topic have tried to answer this question in a broad way. Heidi Hammond's 2012 study used field notes, surveys, and focus groups to research twenty-three high school seniors. The study determined that only 30 percent of the students had read a graphic novel before the study, and that learning about graphic novel conventions increased their comprehension and enjoyment of graphic novels.

An important part of reading occurs when the reader is able to let the book paint pictures in the mind—so that the narrative unfolds in a way not unlike a movie. Some class texts often encountered in English class have amazing potential to let the reader experience epic narrative movement and remarkable visualization, but the syntax, poetic or dramatic form, or contextual demands of the piece make it hard for students to do so. Graphic novel adaptations of these texts often retain the original words, but provide images of characters and actions to help orient readers to the situation being described.

In 2007, James Bucky Carter described classroom practice, arguing for the effectiveness of pairing a modern graphic novel with a classic piece of literature in language arts class. Schraffenberger (2007) argued that a graphic novel adaptation of *Beowulf* allows the students to picture the characters and actions of the well-known Anglo-Saxon poem in a way that enhances the visual descriptions in the poem. Similarly, Fisher and Frey (2007) cite classroom experience to argue for using an entire modern graphic novel in English class.

Other research singles out specific affordances that graphic novels offer. Shipwright, Mallory, Atack, and Demacio's 2010 study indicated that graphic novels might be particularly useful for teaching research literacy skills. They surveyed eighteen undergraduates who reported that "learning research literacy skills through [the graphic novel medium] was enjoyable and the novel format acted as an incentive to read and learn. They indicated that they had made the greatest gains in detecting bias and applying critical thinking skills" (p. 573).

However, not all studies agreed. Schieble's 2011 study engaged in case studies of both preservice teachers and adolescents reading *American Born Chinese* and found that the students "constructed characters' feelings of racial and cultural inferiority as a matter of the individual rather than as a result of institutional patterns of exclusion" (p. 202). In this case, however, it is hard to attribute the failure of the students to ascribe perceptions of social injustice to the graphic novel format when it may be more a reflection of the intent of the particular graphic novel they read, the depth of their engagement with issues of race and equality, or some other factor altogether.

Part of the appeal of graphic novels may be that since we tend to perceive the format as more informal or relaxed, it can be easier for some students to feel a connection to them. Cary Gillenwater, in 2012, looked at two case studies of twelfth-grade English language arts classrooms that "affirmed previous scholarship that the medium of comic books/graphic novels can play a beneficial role in . . . encouraging student ownership of texts."

Graphic novels also provide specific affordances for teachers. Doug Arnett in 2008 conducted semistructured interviews with six middle school, high school, and college English teachers and found that all the teachers felt their students were "very engaged" in the materials (p. 169), that most teachers believed that lower-achieving readers "found more success with a highly visual text" (p. 169), and that graphic novels encouraged out-of-class reading, but that very few of the teachers had ever used graphic novels in their teaching.

Dulaney (2012) engaged in case studies of four English language arts teachers and found that prior knowledge and experience are important for teachers who want to use graphic novels and that graphic novels are well suited for teacher-student partnerships.

Overall, then, graphic novels are useful in teaching English language arts because they can strengthen comprehension skills, help students get images in their minds even when they are reading a classic text where the syntax may make that difficult, help students learn research skills, increase student ownership of texts, and help teachers engage, connect, and partner with their students.

HOW ARE GRAPHIC NOVELS USEFUL FOR TEACHING HISTORY AND SOCIAL STUDIES?

While perhaps the most research has been done about using graphic novels in English class, there is also a growing body of research about using graphic novels in history and social studies classes. Cromer and Clark in 2007 identified several elements that graphic novels have that are necessary for teaching history: time, intertextuality (showing connections between texts), and visual literacy. In 2010, Boerman-Cornell looked at the specific affordances that the graphic novel *The Magical Life of Long Tack Sam* could bring to the study of history. That graphic novel uses embedded timelines, historical photographs, and primary sources to orient readers to the time period being discussed. He also identified the way in which the book is set up as a journey of historical discovery, following the author as she uses historical techniques to find out about her great-grandfather.

In 2013, Boerman-Cornell analyzed George O'Connor's *Journey into Mohawk Country*, a graphic novel that uses the graphic novel format to present the original text of a primary source journal from 1634. *Mohawk Country* uses graphic novel images to present readers with a historical interpretation of how the journal writer's actions would have been perceived by the Mohawk tribes he was visiting. Such an approach has potential to model historical interpretation for young readers.

Another study by Boerman-Cornell in 2011 analyzed three graphic novels to determine the affordances and constraints that the graphic novel format might offer history instruction. He concentrated on three important skills that Wineburg (1991) had identified as being important for history literacy: contextualization, corroboration, and sourcing. In 2015, Boerman-Cornell applied that same analysis to a larger body of work, twenty historical graphic novels.

He found that the graphic novel format allows students to engage in contextualization, corroboration, and sourcing in specific ways that are not possible with conventional texts.

Decker and Castro (2012) conducted an analysis of whether the graphic novel collection of the comic *Unknown Soldier* could engage college undergraduates. They found that the graphic novel's status as a popular art form was a more inviting gateway into deeper historical understanding because it is not a scholarly tome.

Although research is still ongoing, the answer to this question seems to be that graphic novels are powerful tools to enable students to engage in the same sort of analytical reading that historians engage in.

HOW CAN GRAPHIC NOVELS BE USED IN TEACHING SCIENCE AND MATH?

The research on using graphic novels to teach math and science is limited. Tatalovic (2009) describes a variety of science-based graphic novels, but offers little advice about how to use them and no research about their effectiveness. Also in 2009, Barbara Guzzetti engaged in a case study of an eleventh grader and determined that graphic novels would be effective texts in science and language arts. Cooper, Nesmith, and Schwartz (2011) conducted a focus group composed of seven elementary teachers and four college professors, discussing the value of using graphic novels in elementary science and mathematics. Their analysis of the responses "revealed the existence of variance in participants' perspectives of . . . potential benefits, and perceived problems or concerns" (p. 1).

Unlike the research we have seen in English and history, studies of using graphic novels to teach math and science have not yet begun to look at the affordances and constraints of the graphic novel format for those particular academic disciplines.

HOW DO READERS READ GRAPHIC NOVELS?

Scott McCloud, in one of the first books to ever look at the structure of the graphic novel from a scholarly viewpoint, *Understanding Comics* (1994), argued that it is the interaction between comic book panels that hold the key to understanding how we read them. Though there is little research on this topic, McCloud's theory can offer a good picture of what might be going on in readers' minds when they read graphic novels.

Let's take a couple of panels from George O'Connor's best-selling *Olympians* series as an example (see figure 3.1).

So how do you read this? You start in the upper left, of course, with the first panel. Because of the previous pages, you know that the main character, Zeus, is trapped far underground. You see him calling out, "Is anyone here?"

Figure 3.1. From *Zeus: King of the Gods* © 2010 by George O'Connor. *Reprinted by permission of First Second, an imprint of Roaring Brook Press, a division of Holtzbrinck Publishing Holdings Limited Partnership. All rights reserved.*

Above him you see a pair of menacing eyes. But you really aren't actually engaging what makes a graphic novel special until you get to the next panel.

When you get to panel two, your eyes quickly compare the two panels to determine what is the same between them and what is different between them. It is sort of like those games on children's menus at restaurants where the trick is to figure out the differences between the two drawings. In this case you quickly notice several things. First, that Zeus is no longer calling out. Second, instead of one set of eyes, there are now six (although Zeus does not yet grasp this).

When you compare the second and third panels, you see that there are still more eyes and that Zeus has turned and has recognized his predicament. The fourth panel is clearly not directly related to the other panels, and so it might leave you unsure. Obviously you will have to turn the page to understand the context.

As this simple layout illustrates, reading graphic novels requires that readers consider panels (plural) to understand meaning (much as, once young readers become fluent in reading, they read phrases and sentences rather than individual words). Meanings, interpretations, character development, plot changes, themes—all these are conveyed through the interaction of panels with each other, not in a single panel alone (nor even a series of single panels considered individually, one after another).

In fact, as you read more and more pages of a graphic novel, you become aware of panel-to-panel connections that jump pages—where a similar image or layout can tie a scene to another scene even if several pages lie between.

Meaning is also conveyed within panels through the intersection of words and images. Note that is the intersection of words and images, not the sum of them. Multimodal theorists Kress and Van Leeuwen have done extensive analysis about how words and images work together in magazine advertising, where sometimes the words might interact ironically, sarcastically, or supportively with the images. In graphic novels, however, the words are embedded in the image.

Because of this, it is not helpful to try to isolate what aspects of meaning are carried by the text and what parts are carried by the images. Rather, look for how they work together. In panel three of the Zeus illustration, what carries the meaning that Zeus is aware of the menacing eyes is a combination of his body turning (which readers can only see if they contrast it with the previous panel) and his verbal utterance "Uh." Both of these combine to give the impression that he has become aware of his situation.

A great deal of meaning is also conveyed through a kind of special symbolic language that comics and graphic novels use. The shape and size of the word balloons often indicate tone and volume. Speed lines coming out from behind characters indicate the direction and speed they are moving. The size and frequency of the panels can be used to indicate the passage of time with a series of smaller panels close together indicating that time is moving at a frantic pace and a full-page spread often indicating that time has stopped for a moment. As with picture books, shading and color can indicate mood, and the perspective of the viewer can help position the reader emotionally in a given scene.

Of course, all of this is based on McCloud's theory. Researchers are only now beginning to test it. Jimenez and Meyer (2016) found that readers who had a lot of experience with graphic novels looked to the images and other visual elements to give them an understanding of themes, character, and plot. Strong readers of conventional books who had little experience with graphic novels read them primarily by looking toward the text to inform their understanding of story elements. Clearly, then, reading graphic novels is a skill that can be acquired with practice.

If all this seems daunting, it is—but remember, neither you nor your students learned to read a conventional book in a single sitting. As with regular books, learning to read graphic novels takes time—and by having regular discussions with teachers, students can share the insights they are learning as they develop their skills.

OKAY, BUT WHY USE GRAPHIC NOVELS IN THE DISCIPLINARY CLASSROOM?

When asked this question at education conferences, teachers respond swiftly that graphic novels are a great way to engage students. That is true—at least for some students. The students most interested in reading graphic novels in the classroom are those who are already familiar with the format and have read some graphic novels. Students unfamiliar with graphic novels often find their first attempt to read one difficult and occasionally frustrating.

So why do it? As mentioned earlier, this is a multimodal world. An advertisement in a magazine consists of both the image and the text beneath it, and readers must combine the two in their minds to catch the humor or the point of the message. The same is true with reading on the Internet. Most of the time readers look at the image, then look at the separated text, then put the two together.

In the case of graphic novels, however, the text is fully integrated into the images at multiple places. Although research is still investigating how readers read graphic novels, researchers suspect that the process of reading graphic novels is multimodally demanding.

To develop fluency and speed in reading graphic novels, readers must learn to see the image on the page, hold that image in their head as they read the text, make meaning from the intersection of image and text, link that meaning to previous images on that page (and sometimes other pages), and then be flexible enough to alter their interpretation and understanding as they read additional text. Reading graphic novels may be excellent preparation for interpreting other kinds of multimodal formats.

Earlier in this chapter, you learned about affordances and constraints that graphic novels have to offer. Those affordances and constraints are particular to the needs of different disciplines. For example, in mathematics, graphic novels allow diagrams of geometric forms to appear alongside the narrative explanation of the theory or equation being explained (see Ottaviani and Purvis, *Suspended in Language*). In history, multiple sources can present their account of a historical event as a single unbroken narrative, using images of the tellers to distinguish who is speaking when (see Sacco's *Safe Area Gorazde*). In English language arts, an adaptation of Shakespeare can allow students to read the play but also see which character says which lines, and which actions accompany those lines. Chapters 4 and 5 help identify what affordances and constraints graphic novels offer the different disciplines.

HOW CAN ONE TELL THE DIFFERENCE BETWEEN A GOOD GRAPHIC NOVEL AND A BAD ONE?

This question is as difficult as asking how to tell any good book from a bad one. In fact, the answer lies in some of the same considerations: text complexity, appropriateness of the material for the age level of readers, how well the book connects to the content being taught, themes, character development, and so forth—but because graphic novels are multimodal, things tend to get a bit more complicated.

Consider text complexity for example. With a regular book, one might type a sample chunk of text into an online readability website and come up with a grade or age equivalent. Most teachers know to take such a determination with a grain of salt, since the formula that determines the reading level cannot take into account the actual content, nor can it account for differences in interest level.

With graphic novels, all this is complicated because of the synergistic way in which we read graphic novels as a combination of words and pictures. So simply knowing the level of text complexity is not helpful since it doesn't take into account the images and the degree to which they scaffold meaning.

McCloud did an insightful analysis in *Understanding Comics* where he argues that different graphic novels use different proportions of different kinds of panel transitions. These different proportions that McCloud talks about might result in a greater or lesser demand on the reader. In addition, the images that the graphic novel creator provides will scaffold the reader's understanding. For example, facial expressions give the reader a sense of the character's response to an object, word, plot twist, or image. It is also necessary to know the reader's amount of experience with reading graphic novels. An excellent reader of conventional books who is encountering a graphic novel for the first time may find it a difficult adjustment.

When you are considering using a graphic novel in class, you obviously have to consider not only the appropriateness of the written text, but also the appropriateness of the images. Many of the best graphic novels being written today are not aimed at an adolescent and young adult audience, though their subject matter might be perfect for that. A graphic novel might have nothing objectionable in terms of words, yet could have an image that might cause a parent to challenge its use in class.

In terms of overall quality, then, we must consider the strength of the writing, the quality and appropriateness of the images, and how well the graphic novel creator uses the panels to move us through the story. Griffith (2010) suggests a series of questions that might be helpful for teachers to consider when selecting a graphic novel for classroom use: with grateful acknowledgment of her work here is a version of her questions modified for this book:

EVALUATING GRAPHIC NOVELS' USE OF FORMAT

- Does the graphic novel have an interesting cover that depicts the content in a way that is engaging?
- Are the illustrations arranged in a way that offers readers an appropriate level of challenge in following the sequence?
- Do the gutters (the spaces between the illustrations) encourage readers to imagine what happens between them in a way that aids comprehension?
- Does the lettering enhance the reading experience by emphasizing key words in such a way that the reader gets a clearer sense of the voices of the characters and the emphasis of the exposition in text boxes?
- Does the white space between the text, frames, and illustration help readers move through the text, or are the pages overwhelmingly busy?
- What extra appendices, glossaries, or other supplemental material is available at the end (particularly if you are considering a nonfiction graphic novel)?
- Is there a table of contents or index to help readers locate information (again, particularly if it is a nonfiction graphic novel—regular graphic novels rarely have tables of contents)?

EVALUATING GRAPHIC NOVEL ILLUSTRATIONS

- Does the color palette (pastels, primary colors, sepia tones, black and white, etc.) aid the reader in understanding the tone and mood of the story?
- Do the illustrations refine characterization by giving clues as to character emotion, mood, and personality?

- Does the style of art (abstract, impressionist, surrealist, etc.) fit the type of story or information in the novel or does it seem disjointed and out of place?
- Do the illustrations provide enough context and action to keep the reader moving through the story/narrative?

EVALUATING CONTENT FOR GRAPHIC NOVELS THAT ARE FICTION

- Does the graphic novels have three-dimensional characters to whom your students can relate?
- Does the graphic novel have themes relevant to the content you are teaching and to your readers?
- Is the content of the graphic novel relevant and appropriate for your students?
- Are there age-appropriate moral, ethical, or social justice themes that resonate through the story?
- Does the action keep your students' interest and motivate them to continue reading?
- Does the climax of the story develop from the earlier developments in that story?
- Is the conclusion of the story satisfying and thought provoking?

EVALUATING NONFICTION GRAPHIC NOVELS

- Does the graphic novel meet your goals for a specific lesson, unit, or course?
- Is the graphic novel organized in a way that aids comprehension?
- Does the graphic novel encourage ways of thinking that are appropriate to your academic discipline?
- Is the information interesting enough to keep readers actively engaged in the text?
- Are there appealing charts, graphs, and other visual aids to help the reader understand the concepts?
- Do the supporting details explain and develop each main idea?
- Is the content relevant and age appropriate for the understanding level of your students? (pp. 183–184)

The bottom line is, you need to read the graphic novel (much as you would any trade book you were considering using as a supplemental text) for all of the aspects discussed above. Most importantly, consider what the graphic novel can offer your disciplinary classroom in terms of both content and in student engagement in the reading, thinking, and questioning that is specific to your discipline. And that is what the rest of this book is about.

Chapter Four

Graphic Novels in Teaching Academic Disciplines

Graphic novels can supplement, complement, and transform content learning in classrooms. As with traditional trade books, they can provide a more personalized and nuanced understanding of events, characters, and ideas, and can act as a gateway into deeper understanding of concepts and perspectives. Furthermore, with their highly visual format and complex interactions of words and pictures, graphic novels also provide a greater number of opportunities for meaning making that go beyond the printed word.

The term "meaning making" has become more common in conversations between teachers in recent years. It refers to not only reading a text, but the process that occurs in the mind of student-readers as they make sense of that text and connect it to previous understandings and experiences. Incorporating graphic novels may offer meaning-making affordances within disciplines like math and science that may make graphic novels more helpful for some students than a conventionally written textbook or trade book.

The next two chapters explore the ways in which graphic novels can be used to teach disciplinary literacy and cultivate discipline-specific ways of thinking within secondary classrooms. As mentioned in previous chapters, many teachers reach for graphic novels as a teaser to interest struggling readers without taking into account the increased complexity of negotiating pictures and words in tandem to make meaning. Teachers hope that the visual format will help entice reluctant readers or reinforce the weaker comprehension of struggling readers.

While graphic novels can accomplish this, they are capable of far more. Beyond motivation and comprehension, graphic novels can be used to:

- Reinforce comprehension
- Present new content in a different format
- Illustrate difficult or abstract concepts
- Encourage close reading of text
- Foster critical thinking
- Negotiate multiple perspectives of thinking and practice

These texts contain particular formats, language conventions, text features, or text structure that are commonly used in the discipline. For example, science texts often use *nominalization*, where verbs used to describe processes are transformed into nouns. The *process* of evaporation becomes just evaporation. The reader must infer that evaporation is a complex scientific process rather than a single description. A textbook may have an image of a process on the side or on another page; however, graphic novels can unveil disciplinary processes through both image and text.

In the example below, from the graphic novel *Feynman*, the physicist Richard Feynman explains how time and space interact. Behind him is a diagram of the sort one might draw on a classroom whiteboard—but there is a difference. Though Feynman's diagrams change from panel to panel (even as a teacher might add and erase elements as the class goes on), the reader can always back up to that previous diagram if the meaning that is unfolding isn't clear.

Figure 4.1 also demonstrates how image and text are used recursively to show a rather complicated concept—the foundation for Heisenberg's uncertainty principle (that one cannot know both the location and speed of a particle at the same time). Notice how the panels of the graphic novel break up the explanation and include body language, facial expressions, and Feynman's informal voice (panel two, for example, tells the reader that this diagram is simplified and should have four dimensions, but "you can draw that for yourself. I'm not gonna"). The text explains the diagrams, and the diagrams provide visual illustrations for the text.

Within both math and science, graphic novels can lend themselves toward (a) teaching content or (b) acting as authentic literature to help illustrate content. One of the most important affordances in math and science is that graphic novels can show images of difficult-to-understand-or-imagine concepts or ideas.

SCIENCE

While the cartoony, informal nature of graphic novels and the precise, data-driven, formal nature of the domain of science might seem to be incompatible, graphic novels have qualities that make them particularly well suited for

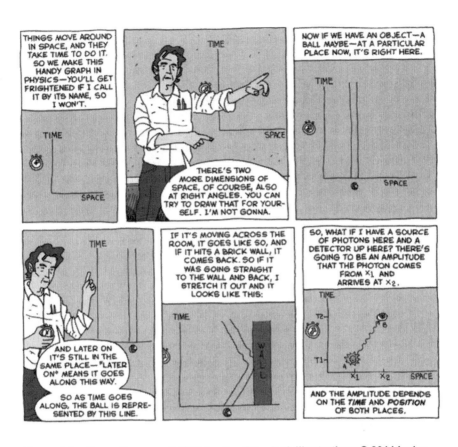

Figure 4.1. From *Feynman* © 2011 by Jim Ottaviani. Illustrations © 2011 by Leland Myrick. *Reprinted by permission of First Second, an imprint of Roaring Brook Press, a division of Holtzbrinck Publishing Holdings Limited Partnership. All rights reserved.*

the abstractions and complexities of scientific education. Perhaps that is why some of the earliest well-received nonfiction graphic novel titles emerged from or were about scientists, for example, the work of Jay Hosler and Jim Ottaviani. Some habits of thinking in science are:

- Questioning
- Hypothesizing
- Model building

The habits of practice in science include:

- Constructing models of scientific processes

- Writing scientific explanations
- Reading nonlinguistic scientific representations

As you can see, particularly with the habits of practice, the visual components of the graphic novel are particularly well suited to aid and foster comprehension of scientific concepts and processes.

Understanding Scientific Habits of Thinking and Practice

As anyone who has engaged in an argument with someone from a very different ideological framework knows, understanding how someone thinks and views the world can be profoundly challenging—and profoundly illuminating. At the core of any good scientist is a basic curiosity about his or her world and a systematic way of exploring it. There are a number of science-based graphic novels that not only convey the history of important scientists and scientific concepts, but also the methods and ways of thinking in which scientists arrived at their discoveries.

For example, *The Sandwalk Adventures: An Adventure in Evolution Told in Five Chapters* (Hosler, 2003) explains Darwin's theory of evolution as fancifully told via two dust mites living in Darwin's eyebrows. While that might seem an absurd setup (and it is), the conceit allows the dust mites to ask the sort of basic questions that students might be embarrassed to ask. It also allows the readers to see in Darwin's responses that—like many scientists—he sometimes works out his ideas in explaining them.

In this way, scientific graphic novels do more than just explain scientific concepts, they model scientific thinking. They pull back the curtain on the way that scientists develop their thinking, making more transparent how the ideas of science are contested by other scientists and how theories develop and change.

Jim Ottaviani and Leland Purvis's *Suspended in Language* (2009) narrates Neils Bohr's life and the development of atomic physics. Ottaviani's *Dignifying Science* (1999) describes the lives and discoveries of famous women in science. Both books explain the concepts these scientists are known for, but also the thinking they followed to reach their conclusions.

Jim Ottaviani and artist Maris Wicks have teamed up to create a graphic novel called *Primates* about three female scientists who studied apes. In the case of *Primates*, one can see the importance of approaching anthropological work without presuppositions and with an open mind, both to methodology and content. Figure 4.2 shows prominent scientist Dr. Louis Leakey in a sort of impromptu job interview with Dian Fossey. She comes into the interview feeling very uncertain because she has no real scientific training, just an intense interest in gorillas.

Leakey responds to Fossey's uncertainty by making clear that what she thinks of as her weakness are actually strengths, and that the most important

Figure 4.2. From *Primates: The Fearless Science of Jane Goodall, Dian Fossey, and Birute Galdikas* © 2013 by Jim Ottaviani. Illustrations © 2013 by Maris Wicks. *Reprinted by permission of First Second, an imprint of Roaring Brook Press, a division of Holtzbrinck Publishing Holdings Limited Partnership. All rights reserved.*

skill in scientific thinking is not encyclopedic knowledge of all scientific fields, but clear eyes and an open mind (though the last panel emphasizes that content knowledge is also important).

Similarly, at the end of *Suspended in Language*, Ottaviani and Purvis provide an example of the importance of considering a variety of solutions to a problem. As a young student, the physicist Niels Bohr is asked to determine the height of a building using a barometer. When his examiner argues that Bohr's answer is wrong, Bohr explains that he did not give the expected answer because there are at least ten other solutions (including comparing the height of the barometer with the height of its shadow proportionate to the length of the building's shadow; or timing how long it takes the barometer, when dropped from the roof, to hit the ground, then working the equation). Bohr's approach is compatible with recent shifts in math curricula to focus on process and innovative problem solving.

All of the above-mentioned titles help demonstrate the way scientists constantly question their world and seek to test and retest their hypotheses about phenomena, all while building on the work of their predecessors and contemporaries. They help make visible to K–12 students the "black box" of thinking like a scientist and becoming more fluent with the discourse of science.

Two very different books by Jim Ottaviani illustrate the importance of scientists' relationships with one another as well. Despite the popular image of the mad scientist laboring away alone in his or her lab (with perhaps a devious assistant or two), scientists are constantly in communication and in relationship with one another. The *type* of relationship, though, can have long-term effects on their work and legacy.

Ottaviani, Schulz, Cannon, and Cannon's book *Bone Sharps, Cowboys, and Thunder Lizards* follows the story of two early American paleontologists who fought with one another for both fossils and recognition in the American West of the late 1800s. Their poor interactions led to a rough start to the early science of dinosaur hunting, particularly in regard to the haste and somewhat sloppy science that resulted. The book includes some of the more recent revelations correcting their mistakes (no more brontosaurus).

In contrast, Ottaviani's biography *Feynman*, which follows the life of quantum physicist Richard Feynman, emphasizes the importance of collaboration in successfully building the atomic bomb. By understanding the modern pressures of first authorship, copyrights, and patents, students can begin to better comprehend the varying demands placed on scientists from their discipline and society. While the dinosaur hunters were motivated by competition with each other, Feynman was energized by conversation and brainstorming with others.

Graphic novels can also teach about the ethical aspects of science as well. In fact, there are a number of studies/articles about using comics and graphic novels in medicine to teach greater humanity and ethics in the application and understanding of science. A profound aspect of science that is left out of most disciplinary literacy studies is the undergirding human element of it all. It isn't difficult to find moments in history where scientific study as "pure" inquiry has led to devastating outcomes like the atomic bomb, where the pursuit of knowledge outpaced the consideration of the application of that knowledge.

Similarly, in medicine, doctors are trained to understand the clinical aspects of disease and health. Without the social or human understanding, though, that clinical information is not enough. Williams's (2012) work explains that the initial point of entry in diagnosis is patient self-report or patient history.

In order to understand the nuances of that self-report, doctors need to have perspective on how individuals understand themselves. Graphic novels can effectively convey the experiences of patients, relatives, and health care providers. Graphic novels might have a particular role to play in the discussion of difficult, complex, or ambiguous subject matter.

Whether documenting a loved one's cancer (*Mom's Cancer* or *Cancer Vixen*) or mental illness (*Epileptic*; *Fun Home: A Tragicomic*; *Swallow Me Whole*; *Mother, Come Home*) or battle with AIDS (*Pedro and Me*), the graphic novel format can help draw a more empathic or visceral reaction to clinical situations. The graphic novel can also provide a counternarrative or nuanced perspective about clinical information. Students will have to synthesize the personal and the clinical in order to attain their own personal understandings of a given situation or diagnosis.

Though it began as a seven-issue comic series from Marvel, the graphic novel *Truth: Red, White, & Black* (Morales & Baker, 2003) tells a complete story that integrates the factual story of syphilis testing on black World War II soldiers with the fictional origin story of the Marvel superhero Captain America. While not historical science exactly, it does provide an interesting mashup of popular culture and scientific history that could provide a point of entry for more resistant students. It engages students in the ethical dilemmas of scientific understanding, the historical contexts in which they are embedded, and the potential outcomes of such work.

Understanding and Representing Scientific Content

There has been a virtual explosion of graphic novels relaying scientific content and important scientific moments from history. Jay Hosler, graphic novelist and scientist, has helped lead the charge—first with *Clan Apis*, which provided a fictionalized narrative of the life cycle of a honey bee, and then on to books such as *The Sandwalk Adventures*, *Evolution*, *Optical Allusions*, and most recently, *The Last of the Sandwalkers*. He uses a narrative model to help relay and unpack the complexities of scientific knowledge from evolutionary theory to the wonders of different types of beetles.

Jim Ottaviani, also a graphic novelist and scientist, has produced about a dozen books, mostly biographical in nature, documenting famous scientists and the eras in which they lived, such as Niels Bohr, Alan Turing, and Richard Feynman. All of these are helpful to students in understanding important scientific concepts and figures, as well as the historical and scientific context from which they emerged.

Particularly helpful to students is the acquisition of skills in reading and analyzing both the visual and literary information found in scientific graphic novels. As cited in Green (2013), "By critically reading visual texts, students become more careful observers," an imperative, highly valued skill in science. There are a number of biology-oriented graphic novels, such as *The Stuff of Life: A Graphic Guide to Genetics and DNA* and *Charles Darwin's On the Origin of Species*, which help depict what is invisible to the naked eye and perhaps more difficult to grasp.

Similarly, the physics-oriented graphic novels, many of which have already been mentioned, provide both visual and linguistic explanations of highly abstract concepts. This double opportunity for understanding material allows students to better access and comprehend the content beyond the confines of traditional print or even print accompanied by the occasional graphic. By either pairing traditional science texts alongside graphic novels, or in some cases using the graphic novel as the primary text, students will continue to develop the multiple modes of understanding the world today.

Finally, the narrative that often accompanies these bits of facts and concepts helps to unify and ground the learning of the students. Human beings are drawn to story, and the seemingly disconnected learning that can happen with standard textbooks finds a broader structure within graphic novels to help build students' schema and understanding. Just as historical fiction can help bring to life seemingly dry and disparate dates, battles, and figures, the unifying aspect of a single graphic narrative can help demonstrate connections and engage students with the content.

Beyond the reading and *consumption* of text, though, graphic novels also allow students to contemplate the *production* of text. Scientific understanding must be communicated to be useful. The transmission of scientific knowledge to the public, whether a public health issue or the sharing of major medical breakthroughs, is an important part of the scientific process. In fact, it is through this public sharing of information and corroboration of information in which science gets tested and validated. Consider the news over the last decade about scientific "discoveries" found to be falsified or questionable because other scientists could not replicate the results.

These kinds of debates can be tricky to convey to a lay audience, however, who may get overwhelmed by the jargon and discipline-specific processes. In a multimodal world more populated with words and images now than at any earlier point in history, graphic novels can help provide another mode of communication that is more accessible. The prevalence of infographics in more recent times indicates this emerging appreciation of picture/text hybridity in illustrating complex concepts.

In Asia (Tatalovic, 2009) and other places, some scientific organizations have even started using comics to help disseminate information about public health issues or scientific methodologies. This accompaniment of text with visuals helps increase the comprehension of technical or complex information by providing multiple avenues of understanding or reinforcing understanding. As twenty-first-century citizens, we are awash in media. Graphic novels can promote abilities to process, engage with, and critically understand media in our schools.

MATHEMATICS

While there are fewer graphic novels in mathematics than in science, there still are several that help illustrate both mathematical content and habits of thinking and practice. Mathematical habits of thinking include:

- Justifying a mathematical claim
- Solving
- Proving

Mathematical habits of practice include:

- Quantitative reasoning
- Communicating with precision
- Persevering in problem solving

Though more difficult in delivering straight mathematical content (e.g., sets of math problems), graphic novels do address mathematical ways of thinking in some novel ways and contexts.

Understanding Mathematical Habits of Thinking and Practice

There is much in common in teaching scientific thinking and mathematical thinking with graphic novels. Comics like *Logicomix* that follow the trials, tribulations, and processes of mathematicians provide a window into understanding how they think and look at the world. In the case of *Logicomix*, the graphic novel explains how theories of mathematics and reasoning are built upon and in correspondence with others' thinking. It demonstrates how math is not merely doing problems in isolation, but a product of both contemplation and calculation. This also further demonstrates how mathematics is not necessarily a fixed point, but an area in flux.

The narrator of *Logicomix*, Bertrand Russell, an influential philosopher and mathematician, critiques and explains famous mathematicians of his time, allowing student-readers to better understand how mathematicians build upon—and tear down—each other's ideas. In a field that seems often clinical and unemotional for students, *Logicomix* demonstrates the passionate methods and sometimes literal madness of mathematicians.

One of the main premises of the book is questioning whether great genius, especially for logicians, is inevitably tied to madness. The book also shows how these mathematicians were products of their time, providing insight into how they shaped and were shaped by the politics of war, culture, and social thought. *Logicomix* also draws neat parallels between the logic of mathematics and the ethics of peace as the story is bookended by two wars.

Similarly, other graphic novels provide a deep social understanding and historical context of significant times and figures. *T-Minus: The Race to the Moon* documents the engineers and mathematicians working in the early days of the space program, and *Suspended in Language* tracks the life of physicist Niels Bohr. While not exclusively about math content, both graphic novels provide historical context and demonstrate the real-life application of mathematical concepts. By showing how mathematicians solve real-world and theoretical problems alike, graphic novels can also motivate students to consider careers in the STEM (science, technology, engineering, and mathematics) fields.

Understanding and Representing Mathematical Content

As disparate as the graphic novel form and mathematical texts may seem, there are actually a number of graphic novels that teach and provide a context for mathematical content. In fact, Gene Yang, of *American Born Chinese* fame, early in his graphic novel career created substitute teaching plans for his calculus class via graphic novel form. His students clamored for them and, much to his chagrin, found them much more accessible than his flesh and blood self.

Yang actually attributed this to the fact that students had control over the flow of information they were receiving. Unlike a "real-time" lecture, students could "pause," "rewind," or stop the lecture at any point they needed to review or process. This may be, in part, why he chose to write his most recent graphic novel series *Secret Coders*, which follows a trio of kids at a prep school who use their math skills to uncover a mystery at their school. While this doesn't directly teach mathematical content, it requires readers to demonstrate their understanding of concepts in order to solve the mystery embedded within the narrative.

The graphic novel *Who Killed Professor X?* is a fascinating blend of murder-mystery, mathematical history, and math problems. In some ways, it is a text fashioned from the dreams of a Common Core math curriculum. The Common Core Standards in math tend to focus on understanding the ins and outs of mathematical functions versus just getting the right answer. This shift away from problems in isolation to a more nuanced understanding of problem solving emphasizes the importance of math application. *Who Killed Professor X?* truly puts forward the idea of math as inquiry and not as just rote learning.

The book is set up as a whodunit to find out who killed the famous mathematician Professor X. The list of suspects is long—all famous mathematicians (within the novel, but also based on real mathematical figures)—and the mystery is solved through a series of mathematical formulas. Each mathematician's location during the time of the murder is determined by solving a mathematical problem in that mathematician's area of expertise.

The use of a narrative format, the humanization of seemingly lifeless historical figures, and the mystery-solving element of solving math problems all help create a very exciting and novel way of understanding math historically and in context. Students are even able to witness the mathematical characteristics of perseverance and reasoning invoked through the mystery format. The two main protagonists have to continually interview suspects and explain their rationale in selecting or disregarding suspects, finally explaining who killed Professor X.

The *Manga Guide to Math* series are also excellent books in a sadly uncrowded field. No Starch Press's series of manga books teach mathematical content through a narrative format. Similar to *Who Killed Professor X?*, the larger story frame delivers the mathematical problems and content. In this manner, students are taught calculus, statistics, probability, and a host of other mathematical concepts.

The *Manga Guide* series has been well received for their content, format, and "real-ish" contexts. Some teachers (Brozo, Moorman, & Meyer, 2013) have chosen to use these manga books in lieu of their own textbooks because of their accessibility. In an effort to push back against quantity over quality, teachers are looking for better ways to teach concepts and not just cover content. However, it is difficult to include enough math content within a narrative story that teachers don't worry students are not getting enough mathematical content for the time spent reading.

One caveat for both math- and science-oriented graphic novels is the increasing number of "graphic introduction"–type books to mathematical and scientific concepts. There are a number of publishers who have hopped on the graphic novel bandwagon and are producing series of books dealing with difficult concepts in a graphic format. Without getting into specifics, it is important for teachers to review critically the books for accuracy, writing quality, and artistic merit. Some of the reader reviews of these series indicate an unevenness of quality or complementarity between text and image or a lack of depth in the narrative. A poor-quality graphic novel will not provide much more (or any) engagement or learning than a traditional textbook, so it is important to consider the value of books individually.

CHOOSING A GRAPHIC NOVEL WITH STEM CONTENT

While in the last chapter we offered some criteria for choosing a graphic novel to use in the classroom, there are some particular considerations for graphic novels used to address goals in STEM classes. Here are some criteria worth considering. Cooper, Nesmith, and Schwartz (2011) suggested that science teachers consider the following aspects when choosing a graphic novel for classroom use:

1. content is accurate and current,
2. content is visible and effectively presented,
3. content is intellectually and developmentally appropriate for the intended audience,
4. text facilitates reader's involvement, understanding, or transfer of science content,
5. theories and facts are easily distinguished and discernable from fiction or fantasy, and
6. text promotes a positive attitude toward science and technology.

Hunsader's criteria for evaluating mathematics texts parallel some of Cooper et al.'s suggestions, but offer some new ones as well:

1. content accuracy;
2. content visibility;
3. developmental appropriateness of content for the book's stated audience;
4. facilitation of the reader's involvement in, use of, and transfer of the content;
5. complement between the story and the mathematics in the story; and
6. resources required for the reader to obtain the maximum benefits of the literature. (as cited in Cooper et al., 2011)

Hunsader also offered a set of criteria for math texts that were told in a narrative or literary style:

1. plot/character development,
2. vivid and interesting writing style,
3. relevancy and appeal of illustrations,
4. developmental appropriateness of readability and interest level for the book's stated audience,

5. complement between the book's plot, style, and illustrations, and
6. presentation of positive ethical and cultural values. (as cited in Cooper et al., 2011)

These are a good start, though here are a few other overall suggestions. First, it is important, above all, that teachers read the entire graphic novel carefully before using it in the classroom to make sure the graphic novel meets the goals for the science or math course, unit, or lesson. Look for ways in which the truth is represented and particularly factual or calculation errors—and remember that in a graphic novel, this is true not only for the words, but for the images, tables, charts, and symbols. Think about whether the way the content is presented is useful and appropriate and how the students (and their parents) are likely to react to that content.

For example, Alison Bechdel's *Fun Home*, mentioned earlier in this chapter, includes depictions of Bechdel's father's struggles with identity, sexuality, and his marriage. Consequently, this graphic novel might be a good choice for some high school psychology classes, but in some communities it might cause so much controversy that the useful content that the graphic novel might bring to students could be lost.

In addition to considering them critically, teachers should look for what each graphic novel offers to students. Consider how well the graphic novel will allow student-readers to interpret words and symbols. Consider how interesting ways of presenting information (for example, how *The Stuff of Life* uses the conceit of an alien explaining human genetics to his leader) may be able to engage students who haven't been able to put the concepts together. Look for ways that mathematical modeling and problem solving may not only engage student interest, but extend it beyond the walls of the classroom and the covers of their math books.

While graphic novels are not a silver bullet for teaching students grappling with difficult concepts and new ways of thinking, they can offer a multifaceted and unique way of engaging students in the STEM fields. As with all powerful tools, though, they must be closely examined for relevance, utility, and meaningfulness. The next chapter will explore the ways in which graphic novels can be used within the humanities.

Chapter Five

Using Graphic Novels in the Humanities

Graphic novels have had a long-standing tradition within the humanities, particularly in continental Europe where they have been embraced fully as a distinct art form. There are major museums for the art of comic books and graphic novels in Brussels, Belgium; Angouleme, France; and Hanover, Germany. In the United States, the combination of writing and images have interdisciplinary appeal and have resulted recently in graphic novels winning prestigious awards for both writing and artwork including the Caldecott and the Newbery Awards.

Still, their use within classrooms is relatively new. While more recently the humanities have embraced them as worthy of study within K–12 classrooms, the phenomenon has probably only gained traction within the last decade or so.

ENGLISH LANGUAGE ARTS

The English language arts (ELA) are perhaps the most natural fit for incorporating graphic novels. Graphic novels have had the longest history within ELA courses, where graphic novels like *Maus* (1980) and later, *Persepolis* (2003) and *American Born Chinese* (2006), were used in countless classrooms (though many other excellent graphic novels remained undiscovered by the education world). More recently, teachers have been discovering a wider range of graphic novels with educational potential.

This may partly originate from the amiable relationship between literature and film (and perhaps also the increased numbers of graphic novels on the market). Many college and even high school courses offer a film studies course housed within the English department, and it is not surprising to find an English class contrasting a film version with a graphic novel. The similarity between the two formats is easy to see.

Teachers may not be wholly aware of the full value of using graphic novels, however. They may think of them as simpler or less sophisticated texts meant for struggling readers or ELL students without fully grasping their complexities or unique affordances, even as graphic novels have had numerous awards bestowed upon them from the Pulitzer (*Maus*) to the National Book Award (*American Born Chinese*) to the Newbery Honor (*This One Summer*). If teachers do not fully acknowledge the complexity involved in reading graphic novels (which can be *more* difficult to read without instruction), their use in the classroom can go awry.

Along these lines, there are two primary ways in which graphic novels can be used in ELA classrooms: (1) as stand-alone texts worthy of independent literary scholarship and analysis, and (2) as complementary texts or graphic adaptations to traditional ELA texts. While there are other ways in which they can be used, such as parts of text sets or book club studies, this chapter will mostly address how they can be used in general whole-class instruction. Graphic novels can be helpful in addressing the ELA habits of thinking:

- Demonstrating a critical stance
- Interpreting
- Reflecting/responding

as well as the ELA habits of practice:

- Reading for literary devices
- Recognizing significance of point of view
- Determining the reliability of the narrator or narrators
- Examining symbolism in literature

Texts like the aforementioned graphic novels would work wonderfully as stand-alone literature, but could also work as complementary texts to more traditional, text-only works in supporting content and skills.

Understanding Literary Habits of Thinking and Practice

There are many ways of understanding the world through literature, and we read literature to better understand society, ourselves, and the world around us. Graphic novels address these ways of understanding and emotional and intellectual connections, insights, and understandings as traditional literary texts.

Take for instance, the poignancy of *Mother, Come Home*. With its washed-out colors and spare drawing style, the graphic novel follows the experience of a young boy dealing with the death of his mother and his severely depressed father. The very lack of ornate language and description provides a window into the raw, quiet pain of the boy and his father.

On the other hand, the harsh, bright colors and semi-exaggerated style of drawing in *The Tale of One Bad Rat* provides a sense of the harshness of the home and street life Helen Potter experiences. Fleeing an extremely abusive home, Helen attempts to make her way in the world and heal from her experiences. Using a design that references the classic Beatrix Potter picture books, *One Bad Rat* persistently contrasts the supposed innocence of childhood with the harshness of the street (and at the same time, shows the street to sometimes be a safer place than the home).

The book is illustrated in a somewhat garish style, which moves into calmer colors as Helen's life becomes happier and calmer. The way *One Bad Rat* uses colors and illustration style can provide a proving ground for students to gain insight into the abstract, invisible ways authors paint, through words and pictures, a very real world full of meaning for their readers.

Another pair of graphic novels that use illustration and story line to demonstrate some complex literary devices are *American Born Chinese* and *Deogratias*. These two books cover very different stories: the cultural negotiations of a Chinese American boy and the psychic break of a Hutu participant/survivor of the Rwandan genocide, respectively. What they have in common, though, are the literal transformations of the teenage protagonists in representing their psychological dissonance.

Jin, in *American Born Chinese*, moves to a new school and struggles with being one of only two Asian American students. He imagines how much greater his social acceptance would be if he were white—more specifically white with curly blond hair and blue eyes. Then midway through the book, he transforms into this Caucasian character, only to be socially humiliated by a visiting cousin from China, a grotesque racial caricature. Deogratias, as a member of the Hutu tribe, participates in various violent acts toward his Tutsi neighbors, and in the aftermath, fueled by alcohol, envisions himself as turning into a dog at night, the beast he truly is.

Both of these stories are fractured through nonlinear timelines and jumps in narrative structure as both characters struggle with reintegrating their understandings of self. While not a substitute for great American classics like William Faulkner's *The Sound and the Fury*, the visual elements of these two complex graphic novels can help provide a more accessible way of understanding multiple narrators and changes in protagonists that may be more difficult with print-only texts.

In this way, graphic novels can help illustrate how writers can represent some very modern/postmodern elements of literature, such as multiple perspectives, unreliable narrators, and complex story structures. They could even be paired with more traditional novels like *Woman Warrior*, whose general Asian American themes are similar to *American Born Chinese*—even interweaving Chinese mythology—as another perspective on a broader genre or topic.

These graphic novels also present opportunities for students to do comparative analysis of literature, pointing out similarities and differences in content, theme, and style, as well as writers' interpretations of similar experiences. The multimodal format of a graphic novel can allow an entry point for students to come at the same themes from a direction that might give them further, deeper insight. There are cues, though, within the visual elements of graphic novels, that further support readers' understanding of nonlinear structure.

For example, in *Deogratias*, the writer uses different-colored frames on the pages to illustrate flashbacks (black borders) and the present (blank borders). Students who struggle with being able to discern changes in narrator or timeline in traditional text will appreciate the visual cues—once they know to look for them, which graphic novelists provide to understand these literary devices.

Graphic novels can also be useful to represent literary devices such as metaphor, allusion, and repetitions as well as structural elements of literature such as sequence and characterization. Consider figure 5.1, a page from *The Plain Janes*.

This scene from the beginning of the graphic novel shows the protagonist, Jane, entering the cafeteria on her first day at a new high school. To understand how graphic novels manage character development, look at the panels again, carefully, one by one, and then ask if Jane should sit with the girls who have made the offer. Even though the girls are smiling, the expression on Jane's face implies a different understanding of those smiles. When the girls talk to her, the smiles on the girls at the table appear "fake" or contrived, and the blonde girl uses language to try to control Jane, not merely to welcome her.

This can serve as an excellent example of subtext—that sometimes it is not what characters say but how they say it that gives us insight into what they are like. In a graphic novel, much of that subtext can be portrayed through facial expressions, body language, and other context clues built into the illustrations.

Graphic novels, and literature in general, can help provide a window into understanding the complexities of people who wouldn't necessarily be seen as sympathetic. In the case of *Deogratias*, it is a boy who participates in ethnic genocide, and in *Cleburne: A Graphic Novel*, a Confederate soldier who fights for the South against the Union.

Figure 5.1. From *The Plain Janes* © DC Comics.

Patrick Cleburne's tale is a less well-known one, but one based on a real individual and historic events. An Irish immigrant who fought alongside the South, Cleburne advocated for the freeing of slaves in exchange for their enlistment in the Confederate army. Even though he abhorred slavery as an institution, he was loyal to the Confederacy, a side not often viewed favorably in most textbooks. Providing such alternative viewpoints helps students build more nuanced and complex understandings of both historic events and the world, as well as the actors within them. We begin to develop more fully realized, three-dimensional understandings of historical actors and not just stock images.

In another example, *Pride of Baghdad* follows the fictionalized account of a pride of lions that escaped from a zoo in Baghdad after the 2003 bombings. Based on a true event, four lions roam the bombed-out city, experiencing freedom ever so briefly. The seemingly trivial event of escaped zoo animals provides a surprisingly human glimpse of the cost and difficulties of war, as well as the innocent lives affected by them. This much simpler and briefer tale still manages to embody many of the much larger themes and complexities of war.

A startlingly different and interesting pairing would be to read this alongside Joe Sacco's *Palestine* or Joe Kubert's *Fax from Sarajevo*. Both of these graphic novels have been front-runners in an emerging form of graphic journalism. Kubert's story follows a Serbian family he is in contact with; Sacco's is a first-person account of his time on the ground in Palestine.

There are a number of other graphic novels that depict experiences during wartime, both fictionalized and true, that can provide insight into the multiple perspectives of actors in these time periods. The notion of choosing, as a writer, to have text alongside illustration—versus more traditional print-only journalism—is one that would be rich to discuss in terms of authorial choice.

Understanding and Representing Literary Content

As indicated in the previous section, graphic novels can work wonderfully alone or paired with other texts. For those more nervous about the actual merit of graphic novels or those looking for a first "toe dip" into their use, pairing them with traditionally more difficult texts—or even in lieu of them—may be a great first exposure.

The *Manga Shakespeare* series has been fairly well received. Because it modernizes and updates Shakespeare's plays, it may be more of a good introduction or parallel text to use rather than a full immersion into the Shakespearean experience, depending on the age of the students. With that said, there are many publishers looking to capitalize upon the interest in graphic novels and new adaptations are released constantly.

It is important for teachers to consider the GRAPHIC format when choosing a text and review what the intended objectives and approaches with using the graphic novel are. If ELA teachers want their students to be familiar with how Shakespeare's plays are traditionally staged, Gareth Hinds's adaptation of *King Lear* (2007b), for example, would work well. Hinds's graphic novel is a heartfelt retelling with the characters in traditional costumes, moving through traditional settings—a great way to give students a sense of the characters and how the play is usually staged.

If teachers are more interested in introducing Shakespeare in a way that might engage student interest with humor, they might try using Ian Lendler and Zack Giallongo's (2014) *The Stratford Zoo Midnight Revue Presents Macbeth*. Lendler and Giallongo offer a humorous summary of the play presented by zoo animals.

If teachers want to show students how Shakespeare is the perfect vehicle for directors to try different interpretations, they might try the previously mentioned *Manga Shakespeare* series. For example, Robert Deas (2008) in *Manga Shakespeare: Macbeth* sets the Scottish play in postapocalyptic Japan. This choice might interest and engage some students (though it might turn others off).

In addition, there are at least three graphic versions of the ancient English tale *Beowulf*—perhaps unsurprising since Beowulf resembles a superhero. Jerry Bingham's (1984) graphic novel adaptation of *Beowulf* portrays Beowulf as a buff superhero sort of guy, complete with bikini-clad women, and could lead to an interesting discussion of whether such an interpretation is faithful to the original work.

Other adaptations (like Gareth Hinds's version) run truer to the original story and language of *Beowulf* than others, but all embody *Beowulf* as a great adventure story. Consider your objectives in teaching *Beowulf* when choosing a version.

These different versions provide layers of interpretation for students to compare and contrast. And because students can return to the graphic novel and think about it (unlike a stage production that they see once, then have to rely on their memory) and since graphic novels are approachable and unassuming (unlike the distracting flash, star power, and soundtrack of a big-budget movie production), students may feel more comfortable analyzing those additional levels of interpretation. This disarming quality may make it easier for students to engage in critical analysis.

It is easy to forget how intimidating literature (or indeed, any academic texts) can be. It may be difficult for students to even imagine thinking critically about an author like William Shakespeare because of the esteem with which their teacher and many other adults hold the famous playwright. The same is true for history, science, and other textbooks. How can we expect students to question that which has been presented to them as the ultimate authority from the time they began school—the textbook?

In contrast, the graphic novel seems to have more in common with the comics in the newspaper or the cartoons on television. Comics and cartoons are formats that children are familiar with and not at all intimidated by. Although graphic novel creators have complained for decades that their work is not taken seriously enough—in this case it is a great advantage. Even in the face of canonical literature—if it is presented in graphic novel format—students may feel more willing to question and criticize that which they see. And fortunately, there is a wide variety of canonical literature that has been adapted into graphic novel format.

I. N. J. Culbard and Ian Edginton have created an excellent adaptation of Sir Arthur Conan Doyle's *A Study in Scarlet* (2010), which might provide an opportunity for students to be able to picture the action and mystery of the story as well as the nineteenth-century syntax. Gareth Hinds's 2010 graphic novel version of Homer's *Odyssey* would be great paired with the original text, giving student-readers the chance to think about what the adaptation cuts and what it leaves in.

Teachers could take a similar approach with Roy Thomas and Miguel Angel Sepulveda's 2008 adaptation of *The Iliad*, which is also very well done. Even literature written in the last fifty years is being adapted. Hope Larson's 2012 adaptation of Madeleine L'Engle's *A Wrinkle in Time* may be an improvement on the original in that it visualizes a story that is sometimes descriptively vague in the text-only version.

All of these are ways that the teacher can extend the influence of his or her teaching without any considerable effort beyond reading graphic novels and making them available to students. This gives student-readers the opportunity to pursue an interest in a way that is engaging and valuable. One of the reasons graphic novels are engaging is that many of them deal with contemporary subjects that are easy for students to make an initial connection with. This brings us to our next section where we see how graphic novels can be used to create personal connections and intertextual connections.

Connections needn't just be with graphic novel adaptations of classics in various fields. Graphic novels can also be paired with other works of literature. For example, the graphic novel *Peanut* by Ayun Halliday and Paul Hoppe describes a high school student who fakes a peanut allergy to gain attention. This work could be read alongside Shakespeare's *Comedy of Errors*, which also deals with what happens when someone misrepresents his or her identity.

Faith Erin Hicks's *Friends with Boys* not only connects to students by describing some of the difficulties the main character goes through as she makes the transition from homeschooling to a large public high school, but it also could link to a book like Robert Cormier's *The Chocolate War* as a way of contrasting two very different transitions into high school.

An intriguing aspect of literature is how emerging writers and works continue to engage with and riff on texts of the past. As the saying goes, "We stand on the shoulders of giants." Contemporary adaptations and updates of Shakespeare are common in film, for example, *Ten Things I Hate about You* and *O*.

In this vein, McCreery and Del Col's *Kill Shakespeare* plays with the idea of William Shakespeare as a demigod whose creations, Othello, Lady Macbeth, Hamlet, and so forth, are at war with one another. Its playful inclusion of Shakespeare's characters and story lines provide a unique perspective in understanding the Bard and his stories. While definitely not Shakespeare, it does draw upon students' understandings of characterization and motivation. Literature is never created in isolation, and *Kill Shakespeare* demonstrates how even contemporary adaptations of the Bard's work can be unique and interesting.

In a more technical way, graphic novels lend themselves well toward helping students unpack more difficult or unfamiliar vocabulary. From the Elizabethan English of Shakespeare to superhero hyperbole, the complementary visual elements of graphic novels can actually make vocabulary comprehension and acquisitions more meaningful and insightful for students than traditional stand-alone print. With an expanded understanding of context clues, students have a broader set of possibilities in analyzing and deciphering new vocabulary.

The dynamic and motivating nature of vocabulary acquisition within a multimodal context has been well documented by researchers like Jim Gee (e.g., 2014). With the scarcity of print in comparison to traditional text, students may be more motivated to determine meanings of new vocabulary from visual context clues instead of just skipping over the words.

The more abbreviated form of the graphic novel, in terms of language and overall length, can also help students in several different ways. First, providing a shorter and more approachable text form for readers is particularly helpful for students who are overwhelmed or even paralyzed by the insurmountable number of words and pages in some texts. Second, graphic novels demonstrate more concise language use, and precision of language choice, in both general writing and adapted texts. Third, they create a more targeted understanding of certain literary devices, like foreshadowing or tone, through the medium of images.

For example, the use of rough weather to foreshadow impending action or to imply a character's ill intentions can provide opportunities for students to infer meaning and unpack nuanced understandings of context without pages of text. This concreteness may well work toward helping students who struggle with comprehension and may benefit from the reinforcement of the image alongside text. This picture/text hybridity hones student-readers' skills in synthesizing information from different aspects of the format (words, pictures, and the intersection of the two).

While reading a graphic novel, students must grapple with any dissonance of meaning between image and text or additional information provided in the images before they continue reading. Students who do not do this automatically or are not taught how to do this by their teachers will continue to struggle as much with graphic novels as with any other traditional text.

Finally, as any ELA teacher has experienced at some point in his or her teaching, sometimes students need help in retaining the basic elements of a story before doing deeper literary analysis. Many ELA teachers show a film adaptation of a classic text before reading that text to help students build a basic schema. Struggling to recall basic story elements limits cognitive capacity for other critical analysis or sophisticated interpretation. Once they can easily remember the story line, students are freed to grapple with their textual understandings. The graphic novel's marriage of the visual and textual increases students' abilities to do more complex cognitive work later.

HISTORY/SOCIAL STUDIES

Other than English language arts, social studies is one of the most fruitful areas for use of graphic novels within the secondary classroom. While social studies mirrors the heavy content and attempted focus on objective fact common to the sciences, it also leans heavily upon narrative and the written word. The interpretation and critical analysis needed in the study, understanding, and representation of history are fully compatible with what graphic novels can offer as a supplemental text. With the inclusion of graphs, maps, and historical documents, social studies draws heavily upon visual elements alongside its dense writings.

The habits of thinking in social studies include:

- Sourcing
- Contextualizing
- Corroborating
- Reconstructing the past

While novice students of history tend to view it as unbiased journalistic objective fact, true historians understand that history is created through the multiple lenses of its actors and a nuanced understanding of the happenings of the times.

The habits of practice in social studies include:

- Reconciling competing accounts of the past
- Identifying causal relationships

In fact, a significant amount of the negotiations involved in the study of history deal with critically comparing and analyzing the multiple viewpoints to come up with a coherent and relatively whole story. This may involve looking at primary and secondary sources, examining various artifacts, and getting multiple perspectives—all affordances graphic novels can offer to the social studies teacher.

Understanding Historical Habits of Thinking and Practice

An oft-repeated adage within history is "History is written by the winners." This saying points out that history is more a representation of one side's experiences than an unbiased documentation of events. Perhaps that is why so many of the habits of thinking in history are about unpacking the origins and contexts of sources, as well as fact-checking and comparing them to others.

One of the most well-known and long-used graphic novels is Spiegelman's *Maus*, which follows the story of a journalist documenting his father's experience in the concentration camps during World War II. What may be most striking initially about this graphic novel is Spiegelman's deliberate choice to illustrate its human actors as animals—specifically the Nazis as cats, the Jews as mice, and the Poles as pigs.

Despite the fact he is presenting the story as autobiographical in nature, by representing the various characters as animals, Spiegelman makes clear to the reader that this is his personal interpretation of his father's perspective on the events depicted. The reader understands that Spiegelman is relaying specific messages through his illustration choices. In other words, *Maus* clearly shows that there is a perspective or understanding the writer/illustrator brings to the historical events beyond a simple retelling.

This marriage of the personal and the political through narratives of conflict seems to be particularly well suited for graphic novels. So much of history and its documentation is a strange blend of the intensely personal and individual with the impersonal and faceless. The graphic novel, with its dual visual and narrative elements, provides a perfect platform to juxtapose multiple access points of understanding.

The sheer number of graphic novels depicting war and conflict seems to confirm this: *Maus, Echoes of the Lost Boys of Sudan, Deogratias, Fax from Sarajevo, Palestine*, and *Persepolis*, to name a few. These graphic novels present opportunities for students to understand larger conflicts through the people who navigate them.

The visual matter in history textbooks often attempts to provide this window into the personal through photographs and other artifacts, alongside the much drier list of dates, events, and figures. However, students often tend to ignore these in favor of following the main narrative flow of the text. The graphic novel form helps readers process both texts and images dually frame by frame and does so within a single narrative flow rather than through easily ignored sidebars.

In using graphic novels to teach conflict, there is great potential of teaching how conflicts are more nuanced and complicated than just the simple "good guy, bad guy" rhetoric we've more recently fallen into. Some of these ideas have already come up in the previous section. From Yang's *Boxers* and *Saints* to Modan's *Exit Wounds* and Stassen's *Deogratias*, graphic novels have provided a meaningful and moving way to understand the perspective of those who have been on the traditionally voiceless side of history.

Yang's *Boxers* and *Saints* looks at the Boxer Rebellion (as titled by Westerners). The two volumes depict the experiences of two characters on opposite sides of the conflict, the converted Christian Chinese and the insurgent "boxers" fighting against Western imperialism. The book describes how both opposing sides were highly personal and made sense to those involved. And though the outcomes are tragic overall, the narrative structure and visual elements of the intertwined stories allow students to gain insight into a very lively and personal understanding of these events—one that encourages them to grapple with the contested nature of history.

In terms of historical thinking and agency, to study history means that students must think through the ways in which individual people chose to act under given circumstances (Clark, 2013, p. 492). Graphic novels portray seemingly impersonal and anonymous conflicts in very intimate and individualized ways. In them, history is not just something that happens but is created by people—just like the students reading them—doing what they think is right.

Personal connections are not only important only in literature. Graphic novels can make history and other subjects come alive, too. While it is unlikely that any high school students today have been in a similar situation, *Incognegro* allows student-readers to put themselves in the shoes of the reporter and think of the early civil rights movement in a much more personal way.

Mat Johnson and Warren Pleece's *Incognegro* tells the story of a light-skinned African American reporter from Harlem who attends lynchings in the south and then publishes photos and names of those who were in attendance. After a close call, the reporter decides to quit, but his editor convinces him to take one more assignment—because the reporter's half brother is in jail and expected to be lynched.

Matt Phelan's *Bluffton: My Summer with Buster* combines history and literature in the tale of a boy growing up in Muskegon, Michigan, where his parents rent summer cottages. Each summer a traveling vaudeville/circus comes for a rest, and the main character makes the acquaintance of a young boy named Buster. Only at the end of the graphic novel do readers find out that Buster is actually Buster Keaton, the famous film star. Such books allows students to make a personal connection to historical figures and times.

One excellent example of how graphic novels can convey both content and habits of thinking and practice in history is *Abina and the Important Men*. Taking part in the late nineteenth century on the Gold Coast, the story is a straightforward narrative of a young West African girl, Abina, who sues her master for enslaving her. Broken into five parts: (1) The Graphic History, (2) The Transcript, (3) Historical Context, (4) Reading Guide, and (5) Abina in the Classroom, this graphic novel is a practice in historical thinking and action.

It begins with the product, the graphic story of Abina's story and court trial. It then moves to the primary document from which the story originates—the full court transcript of the trial; pulls back to provide the historical context of the period and area; explains the rationale, thinking, and processes of the writer and illustrator in synthesizing all of this information; and finally provides some ideas for teachers on how to use the book.

While the opening graphic history section is a window into a little-known experience, the accompanying sections provide an equally intriguing glance into how historians work with multiple sources to synthesize and produce their understandings of historical periods. Elements like the court transcripts, graphs and maps of information from the period, as well as other primary source documents, allow Getz and Clarke to make explicit their process in bringing this story to life.

The transparency with which they divulge their processes and biases, ultimately implicating the interpretations and biases of *all* presented histories, is particularly important in demonstrating to students how history is not a static or complete thing but a living, breathing, and incomplete discipline. In fact, the authors' allusion to Abina as being part of a "people without history" points out how so many voices have been left out of the history presented in schools because of lack of access to literacy, documentation, and preservation, not to mention the biases and interpretations of historians themselves.

Understanding and Representing Historical Content

The call for social studies teachers to incorporate more trade books and narrative texts often falls on deaf ears or is turned aside with mutterings of content to be covered and not enough time. Yet, graphic novels, with their abbreviated text and increased likelihood for student engagement, can work well in the social studies classroom to help students better understand and contextualize events. The affordances of graphic novels in being able to address the complexity of reconstructing the past and understanding perspectives can further be witnessed in the wealth of graphic novels that explore marginalized populations' experiences.

While there could definitely be more, there is a relatively rich selection within African American history: *Nat Turner, Incognegro, Malcolm X* (there are two versions as of this printing), *Strange Fruit: Uncelebrated Narratives from Black History, The Silence of Our Friends*, and *March*. Most of these take place during or before the civil rights movement, with John Lewis's *March* being the most contemporary within the list.

March provides an excellent framing of contemporary and historic events through the real-life experiences of Congressman John Lewis, who participated in the march on Selma and currently serves in Congress. The story itself also uses flashback as a device for Lewis to talk about both his past experiences and his present-day career. *Strange Fruit* takes a slightly different tack in detailing the achievements of the lesser-known or "uncelebrated" African Americans in history. As it is a compilation of shorter biographical sketches, it lends itself well toward using the book in its entirety or as a supplement.

While there are a handful of Asian American graphic novels, *American Born Chinese* being the most well known, sadly there are very few graphic novels suitable for the classroom with Latinx or Native American protagonists. This reflects a much broader issue within history textbooks and their lack of equitable representation.

The late Howard Zinn's history text *A People's History of the United States* looks to remedy the unwritten, uncelebrated, and often unknown histories of the people on America's margins. This densely packed book is often seen as *the* counternarrative to the traditional school version of American history. Its length, however, is often enough to scare away many readers.

His more recent graphic adaptation *A People's History of American Empire* attempts to provide a more illustrated, abbreviated, and student-friendly version of his broader text. Both of these texts have been critiqued by some as being anti-American and biased toward the left, but they make an excellent complement to a traditional history text or other book in order to engage students in a discussion of perspective and bias. The pairing of texts would provide a particularly discipline-specific opportunity for students to engage in using the habits and practices of historians to construct their own understandings.

Finally, a few panels from the graphic novel *Journey into Mohawk Country* provide a particularly interesting opportunity for students to synthesize their understanding between the written and the visual. George O'Connor provides an illustrated accompaniment to the actual travel journals of Har-men Meyndertsz van den Bogaert, a Dutch trader to the Americas from the mid-1600s.

Throughout the book, O'Connor combines the original words of the diary with his own images to fill in the gaps with educated guesses at possible interpretations of the words. O'Connor makes the argument that the reason that van den Bogaert and his traveling companions had no luck in increasing Dutch trade with the Mohawks was their cultural insensitivity. In some panels, it is easy to see the connection between the words in the diary and O'Connor's depiction. In other panels it is a bit of a stretch. Consider how students might reconcile or synthesize differences between the written and the visual in figure 5.2.

There is nothing in this part of the text of the diary to imply that van den Bogaert played a mean trick on the Mohawk hunter's dogs—though the visuals certainly change the way we feel about the main character. While O'Connor does not stray from the actual written word of van den Bogaert, he provides quite a bit of additional information through the illustrations that provide a different context or understanding of what may have been going on beyond the written word.

This potential conflict or contrast between words and pictures requires students to grapple with their own understanding of what may have happened. It also helps to underscore that written documents by dominant groups may not have given the full story, and historians must work to fill in these gaps.

While O'Connor could be seen by some as heavy handed in his interpretation of van den Bogaert's written words, Sacco's more journalistic style (e.g., *Palestine*), tends to avoid a single, linear narrative; rather, "he gives voices to multiple viewpoints and fractions, having no pretension whatsoever that any one of them represents a dominant or mainstream version" (Juneau & Sucharov, 2010, p. 180). In *Palestine*, Sacco represents many different story lines and the graphic novel is much more attuned with representing others' stories than in representing his narrative.

By making more transparent the multiplicity of sources, forces, and potential conflicts of meaning, graphic novels allow students to grapple with interpolating and extracting their own meaning like historians. In this manner, graphic novels can "provide an accessible resource for readers to engage with the choices of historical agents and the structural forces they faced, and to interpret the historiography of historical accounts in the history classroom" (Clark, 2013, p. 504).

Figure 5.2. From *Journey into Mohawk Country* © 2006 by George O'Connor.

CONCLUSION

Whether representing disciplinary content or helping to develop discipline-specific ways of thinking and practices, graphic novels provide ample opportunities for students to engage in meaningful ways with their learning. Their picture/text hybridity offers very unique opportunities for teaching and learning, whether using them as primary, complementary, or supplementary texts. The next chapter explores in greater detail the affordances of graphic novels and picture/text hybridity.

Chapter Six

Picture/Text Hybridity

One of the things that sets graphic novels apart from regular text novels, textbooks with photos, charts and maps, and even children's picture books is the way that, in graphic novels, the text and images intertwine so closely. The graphic novel format uses narrative boxes to embed the narrative directly into the image panel, uses text balloons to connect individual utterances with the faces of people saying them, and provides the opportunity for speech to continue even in a panel with an image that shows what the speaker is looking at.

In the GRAPHIC framework, the effectiveness of picture/text hybridity is something that teachers should consider when selecting graphic novels to meet specific curricular goals, and when planning instruction and opportunities for critical student responses. The hybridity of pictures and text is really the language of the graphic novel.

Recall from the first chapter that picture/text hybridity is the way the words and images in a graphic novel interact to make meaning. When you see a billboard on the highway, you see the image and read the text; often the text is a clever turn of phrase that depends upon the image for you to get the joke. Remove either the image or the text and the sign would not make any sense.

Graphic novels, however, take this to a whole new level because, instead of a single image and a single line of text, the graphic novel format allows multiple texts to be embedded in each image/panel, and multiple image/panels to be embedded in each page.

So unlike the billboard, where one can quickly digest the image and the text and understand the two together, with a graphic novel, the reader has to digest the overall picture and then consider how the facial expressions and body stances of the characters depicted affect the way they are saying whatever is in their speech bubble. The reader also has to be aware of changes from panel to panel that affect the way the characters' lines are to be read and the way the reader is to interpret the narration boxes.

Picture/text hybridity works in at least three ways:

1. Within panels
2. From panel to panel
3. In recurring panels

Picture/text hybridity *within panels* refers to the way the pictures and text within a particular panel build meaning in the interaction between them. Consider figure 6.1. In the first panel of this page from Ben Hatke's *Mighty Jack*, there is the most basic kind of picture/text hybridity within panels. Jack is saying, "Maddy?" The image shows Jack in the middle of a wide-open space with a lot of people walking about. The combination of the text and the image leads readers to suspect that Jack is looking for someone.

The second kind of picture/text hybridity *is panel to panel.* Look at the first four panels from that page in a series. The picture/text hybridity within each panel is reinforced by the way each panel ties together. If readers tentatively conclude from the first panel that Jack is looking for someone named Maddy, the second panel confirms that, by the text "Wh–where—" and the image of Jack pressed between people with a look of panic on his face and the focus of his eyes that seem to be looking for someone.

So it is not just that the intersection of image and text combine within the panel—but the recurrence of character, location, expression, and textual content from one panel to the next reinforces our conclusion from the first panel. The third panel reinforces it again, but moves the story ahead. Jack says, "Maddy!" with an exclamation point rather than a question mark, and the image shows his gaze focused on (and presumably his body moving toward) a person in the background. The intersection of text and image tells us that he has found Maddy and that the skinny girl in glasses might be her.

The next panel gives us a closer shot of both of them. The text "There you are" confirms that this is who Jack was looking for, and the text that follows, "What were you doing? What if—," combines with Jack's facial expression and body language to tell us that he is angry.

The third kind of picture/text hybridity *is recurring panels.* This happens when a particular image (a vantage point, character stance, or iconic visual) shows up at a critical moment in a story, then later shows up at a similar moment later in the story, creating a kind of visual echo that repeats the moment of intersection between image and text in a different context.

Several pages later in the story, after Jack and Maddy have resolved this part of the story line, Jack might appear in a panel layout similar to the first panel; only instead of saying, "Maddy?" he might be saying, "Oh, no. Not

Figure 6.1.　From *Mighty Jack* © 2016 by Ben Hatke. *Reprinted by permission of First Second, an imprint of Roaring Brook Press, a division of Holtzbrinck Publishing Holdings Limited Partnership. All rights reserved.*

again." In that case both the images and the text would be carrying the reader back to that earlier point in the story.

Another way of distinguishing between different types of picture/text hybridity is to think about the ways the words and images interact in terms of meaning. While not necessarily a complete list, images and text can interact in at least these three ways:

1. Completing the meaning
2. Irony or sarcasm
3. Parallel tracks

When image and text work together to each provide a piece of the meaning (as in the panels we just discussed from figure 6.1), we might say that they are *completing the meaning*. This is probably the most common sort of picture/text hybridity and it is what makes the magic of graphic novels work. Accomplished graphic novel readers become proficient at combining the meaning pieces from image and text. It is this that makes the characters in graphic novels seem to speak. Though researchers are only just beginning to investigate what goes on in the mind when a reader reads a graphic novel, this type of picture/text hybridity may be the easiest and the quickest to read.

Some picture/text interactions involve *irony or sarcasm*. Return to figure 6.1 and look at the last two panels. Piper says, "She's fine, Jack" and "Trust me." However, since the reader knows that Jack has never met Piper before and since Piper's casual disregard of Jack's concern for Maddy is evidenced in his casual body language, the reader might recognize a disconnect between the image and the text. Yet the intersection of text and image is still driving the meaning. This sort of picture/text hybridity may require more thought from the reader and may slow down the reading process.

Finally, the least common type of picture/text hybridity is *parallel tracks*. Parallel tracks are rare, but occur when the text is telling one part of the story and the images are telling another part and the two stories intersect from time to time. This is perhaps closest to a form of panel-to-panel transition that Scott McCloud (1994) identified as aspect-to-aspect, in which the connections between panels are hard to identify. McCloud argues that these sorts of stories are most common in graphic novels originating in Asian nations.

There is another dimension to picture/text hybridity, though. How readers interpret the interaction between images and texts also depends on the context in which they are reading. Let's consider some examples.

Amy teaches high school social studies. Her history textbook tends to speak of broad historical movements and sweeping generalities that make it harder for her students to dig into the lives of the real people who form history. Her students also tend to view textbooks as authoritative fonts of truth and knowledge, and Amy is having trouble getting them to consider the possibility that the textbook is written from a particular perspective and that it positions its readers in a particular way due to an inherent bias. Can the picture/text hybridity in graphic novels help?

Eric teaches freshman geometry. This year he has larger classes than usual—his smallest one has thirty-one students in it. He has a handful of students who are very gifted in math, but who also seem bored in class. He wants to engage them in something fun, but he doesn't want to burden them with a ton of extra work. He wants something they can dig into in class to replace the introductory unit the rest of the class will work on for the first month of school.

He has tried using the classic book *Flatland*, but in spite of some illustrations in that book, the students have a hard time picturing it. Could the picture/text hybridity of graphic novels make a difference?

Teri has looked over recent testing data and has concluded that although her sophomore anatomy students are very good at memorizing definitions, they are having trouble understanding how biological processes fit together. They especially struggle with getting the big picture of genetics.

Teri has assigned chapters in the textbook, discussed them in class, and has even given them simulation exercises involving different genetic strains of bean plants. Her students seem to understand each part of this, but are having trouble putting the pieces together. On the tests, they cannot apply their knowledge to different genetic situations. Terri has heard of some graphic novels about evolution and genetics. Could using them make a difference?

When Wyeth graduated and got his first job teaching high school English, he figured it was a dream come true. He couldn't wait to introduce his students to all his favorite authors and poets—especially Shakespeare—and watch as those writers had the same kind of deep personal impact on his students as they did on him. Now, five years into teaching, he is ready to give up on Shakespeare. His students complain about it bitterly.

Wyeth thinks it would help if he could actually take them to a play to see Shakespeare acted out, but the district doesn't have the money for that. He has thought about showing them a film version, but that would take up five class periods, and he doesn't have that kind of time to spare.

Could a graphic novel version of *Hamlet* come close to what students would see on the stage? Could the picture/text hybridity let students picture the characters? Could it help his students connect the characters and themes of literature to their own lives?

The answer to all of these questions is maybe, but it depends on the graphic novel. Graphic novels, just like trade books, vary in quality, particularly in their ability to make that crucial picture/text link. There are several educational comic books on the market now that are examples of poor picture/text hybridity. In those comic books what the character is doing in the image has only a casual connection to the exposition happening in the image.

Suppose there is an image of an Indiana Jones–looking figure driving a Land Rover on the edge of a cliff and the speech bubble coming from his mouth says, "The word paleontology comes from an ancient Greek word meaning old or ancient. So paleontology is the science of studying life in the geologic past, usually by studying fossils." In this case, the creators of the comic book are trying to add excitement to a rather dull definition by showing a dramatic moment—but that image is not adding anything to the definition at all.

In other graphic novels, one might turn to a random page and see a character say, "Wow, I am really surprised at that!" and the image shows a shocked face. In this case, the image is at least affirming the words, but in this case as well, the graphic novel isn't making the most of the special relationship between the images and the words.

But seeing whether the images and words work together generally is only the first part of figuring out the picture/text hybridity potential for a graphic novel. Graphic novels also have some affordances in picture/text hybridity that are particular to teaching content. While this chapter's focus will be on the use of graphic novels in a general overall way, it will also frequently acknowledge the necessity of differentiating these principles for each academic discipline. Specifically, the chapter will consider how picture/text hybridity can do the following:

- Build our students' background knowledge
- Extend our teaching outside of lesson plans and classrooms
- Provide additional depth and perspective beyond what textbooks offer
- Create personal connections and intertextual connections
- Provide multiple perspectives
- Provide a visualization of abstract concepts or processes

In looking at each of these affordances of graphic novels and what they require of teachers, readers may be able to answer the questions that Amy, Eric, Teri, and Wyeth have—and the ones that readers will encounter in their classrooms as well.

USING PICTURE/TEXT HYBRIDITY TO BUILD OUR STUDENTS' BACKGROUND KNOWLEDGE

Remember Amy, the social studies teacher? Her students are beginning a unit on the Middle East. There is a huge gap between what Amy knows about the Middle East and what many of her students know. Although a handful of them have cultural connections to those regions, all of her students lack knowledge of geographical, cultural, historical, sociological, economic, and religious aspects of that region.

They might not know where Jordan is, what the different religious beliefs of people living in Iran are, how the history of the formation of Israel and Palestine affects the relationship of Israelis and Palestinians, nor a thousand other aspects of understanding a very dynamic geographical area.

Amy faces two significant difficulties. First, in teaching this content, it is difficult to figure out where to start. To understand each aspect, Amy's students will need all the other pieces. Textbooks usually begin with an introduction that lays out the basic concepts of the topic at hand. After giving a simplistic summary, textbooks typically address each of the components of whatever is being studied in gradual detail that builds upon itself. And on the face of it, this seems like a logical approach.

Anyone who has ever taught, however, knows that textbooks rarely engage student interest in a significant way. The slow and gradual approach to gaining background knowledge is actually not the way students usually learn things.

If you have never followed hockey before, but you begin to develop an interest in it, it is probably not because you picked up a copy of *An Introduction to Hockey* off the shelf. More likely you went to a game with a friend or spouse; your child, nephew, or niece has joined a team; or perhaps the local professional team is having a really good season and you are drawn in by the excitement. Similarly, textbooks composed of generalities, summaries, and overviews—if they are the only text students encounter—may fall short, primarily because, although they make logical sense, the slow pace and lack of interesting narrative detail rarely engages students.

Second, simply memorizing disconnected facts will do little to give the students real understanding. Even if Amy can teach her students to fill in the names of countries on a map, that information is not helpful unless they understand the significance of Jordan's location to how it relates with its neighbors. Even if her students memorize the characteristics of Sunni and Shia religious communities, they may not be able to connect those religious beliefs with politics or economics. In order for her students to be able to hold on to and use that information, they need to have a knowledge that is situated.

James (2014) Gee has written about the importance of situated knowledge. He uses the analogy of a video game as an example of situated learning. When people play video games, they enter a situation where the challenge they are trying to overcome is embedded in an entire world. This means that problems can be almost as complex as those we deal with in everyday life. Actions result in reactions—some intended, others not. The player learns skills on a need-to-know basis. And often the whole experience, like life, can be framed as a coherent narrative.

Books have been described as the first virtual reality machines. When readers read a book they truly enjoy, they get lost in another world. Psychologist Mihaly Csikszentmihalyi has studied the phenomenon of people getting lost in moments of intense focus or activity and refers to it as *flow* (1997). When you are in flow, you lose track of time and often do not hear when someone calls your name. Partly this is because, when reading a novel, you are, along with the main characters, in a situated story. The problems that the protagonists deal with are part of complicated and complex situations, which you feel like you must deal with, too.

This is also partly why trade books, when used in conjunction with textbooks, are so effective in helping students develop background knowledge. The students in Amy's social studies class might find that a novel told from the point of view of an Israeli boy in love with a Palestinian girl helps them connect deeply with the political, social, and religious landscape of those nations because they develop an intense situational interest in that relationship (which may remind them of some aspects of their own lives).

There has, as yet, been no research into the degree to which graphic novels allow readers to enter the flow state. The authors' experiences suggest that some graphic novel readers seem to enter the flow state quickly and deeply. This may be in part because the combination of images and text can engage both the visual part of the imagination (as movies do) but also allow the reader to see into the mind of the character using the linguistic part of the imagination (as in regular text novels).

Such graphic novels allow the reader to pick up content knowledge in an all-at-once manner. To return to Gee's video game analogy, a typical video game does not begin with a lengthy introduction that explains the sociopolitical basics endemic to the setting of the game. Rather, the player jumps directly into the action and picks things up along the way. Books, and particularly graphic novels, also do this.

Picture/text hybridity allows graphic novels to plunge readers into a fully immersive experience (like the video games in Gee's research). A graphic novel can show background knowledge literally in the background.

Joe Sacco's *Footnotes in Gaza*, for example, shows the reader a complete image of life in Gaza, including the distinctive neck scarves that people wear, the slapdash nature of most habitations, the expressions on people's faces when they encounter a neighbor wounded in a skirmish. Much of this background material is present in almost every panel, but not directly commented on at first.

Sacco's narrative (told through his voice in narration boxes, and through the voices of those he interviews in speech balloons) proceeds more methodically, explaining only what is germane to each part of the narrative. In this way, a graphic novel can immerse students wholly into a particular situation through the images while reinforcing those images at the same time with the text.

Amy might also find Harvey Pekar's *Not the Israel My Parents Promised Me* useful, particularly in teaching her students to think critically. In it, as in all of Pekar's nonfiction graphic novels, we get to hear an interesting combination of a range of opinions. Pekar's honest and often grumpy commentary is often counterpointed by those with whom he talks, who sometimes disagree with him. This picture/text hybridity (which often tends toward irony and sarcasm) allows us to see skeptical facial expressions in both Pekar and those he is talking with. This might encourage Amy's students to learn to question the different opinions being put forth.

Each of these graphic novels situates the reader in the midst of the complicated sociopolitical world of the Middle East, allowing the student-reader to pick up background knowledge in an engaging way.

One way Amy could build her students' background knowledge quickly would be to break them up into jigsaw groups: have each group pick a book, read it, then engage in a guided whole-classroom discussion with each of the groups weighing in on particular questions or issues. Though the examples here are specific to history, graphic novels can be used in similar ways to help students develop background knowledge for nearly any subject.

USING PICTURE/TEXT HYBRIDITY TO EXTEND OUR TEACHING OUTSIDE OF LESSON PLANS AND CLASSROOMS

Remember Eric's math class? Eric recognized that there were several students in his class who might have benefited from an extra challenge or two. Stephen Krashen (2004) finds that reading is least satisfying for students when it is assigned, because they have no choice about what to read and no choice about what to do with what they read. In contrast, when students are given a choice of what to read (even between three or four books on the same topic), given the opportunity to pursue something they have interest in, and even given the chance to determine how they will be assessed, they tend to be deeply engaged both in and out of the classroom.

Neither Krashen nor any other researcher to date has considered whether having a choice of formats similarly gives students a sense of agency that increases their motivation, but one would assume that logically this would be true. Not every reader enjoys the picture/word synthesis in graphic novels, and not every graphic novel is worth reading, but the hybridity of words and pictures, and the excitement and innovation that format engenders, means that there are a lot of options available to disciplinary teachers.

If students are pursuing a topic or area that interests them on their own initiative, such research will likely be enjoyable for them. As we have seen in chapters 4 and 5, teachers need to know the objectives specific to their discipline and also need to be familiar with the graphic novels that will effectively use picture/text hybridity to meet them.

For example, Eric wants to engage his stronger students in out-of-class reading. He needs to consider his objectives in doing so, however. As we saw in chapter 4, graphic biographies of mathematicians like Bertrand Russell (*Logicomix*) or physicist Niels Bohr (*Suspended in Language*) could engage his students' deeper interest in the field and extend students' identities as mathematicians. Graphic novel mysteries like *Who Killed Professor X?* give students the chance to solve geometry and algebra problems in the context of an interesting story. This can be useful in some contexts as review, or in other contexts for students to work ahead.

If Eric can build himself a collection of math-related graphic novels covering a range of biographical subjects, fictional puzzle graphic novels, and explanatory graphic novels, he will be in a better position to capture the interests of students who find reading at the intersection of words and pictures an enjoyable (and sometimes exhilarating) experience.

It would be a mistake to think that graphic novels are only useful for supplemental reading for Eric's gifted or motivated students, however. Regular students and struggling students can also benefit from the picture/text hybridity of graphic novels. Think about how a gifted teacher explains a new concept to students. Typically such a teacher uses an interactive whiteboard, a physical object, or even hand gestures to give shape and form to the concept he or she is describing. Graphic novels can do the same, only with much more detailed pictures.

Consider the graphic novel version of William Ayers's book *To Teach*. At one point in the book, Ayers is explaining how curriculum is more than just a list of facts and subjects and lessons, but is more a matter of learning to ask questions, to think critically, to work with each other, and so on. With each aspect of Ayers's expanded definition of curriculum, artist Ryan Alexander-Tanner provides a different illustration, all centered in the classroom whose students and teacher we have been following since the beginning of the book.

When education students struggle with the expanded definition in word-only format, they understand it much more fully when they see the images. In that case, some students who might be considered academically stronger might not need the graphic novels as much as some students who struggle with the concept.

While math serves as a good example, different high school disciplines will use graphic novels to extend learning in very different ways. For example, one teacher, Michael C., teaches high school art. He has used grants and some of his own money to buy enough graphic novels that every worktable in his art room has a small shelf of them. Students are welcome to check them out and take them home anytime. Michael C. does not assess their reading of the graphic novels nor require them to write book reports. Rather, the students see the graphic novels as resources to give them ideas of style, image, and concepts they can use in the art they are creating.

For Michael C. and all teachers, however, what is critical is that they be as familiar as they can with the graphic novels on the classroom shelves, and with his students, so that they can match interests, needs, and objectives.

USING PICTURE/TEXT HYBRIDITY TO PROVIDE ADDITIONAL DEPTH AND PERSPECTIVE BEYOND WHAT TEXTBOOKS OFFER

Wyeth, the language arts teacher mentioned at the beginning of this chapter, recognizes that graphic novels might be able to take his students beyond where the script of a Shakespeare play might be able to take them. He may not realize, however, that the intersection of words and pictures in graphic novels can provide additional depth and perspective beyond what students can get from their textbooks.

Wyeth is interested in using graphic novels to fill in for something that a script doesn't do on its own: picture the action. As mentioned in chapter 5, there are many graphic novel adaptations of Shakespeare's plays, going all the way back to collected classic comics in the 1970s. Though they vary greatly, all of them picture the action of the plays so that students can see it the way it might look onstage. Students can see (and easily distinguish) the characters, their actions, their emotions, the settings, and the moods.

In addition, because they are composed of drawings as well as words, graphic novels can offer close-ups and long-distance perspectives. Because of the picture/text hybridity, they can also make clear when characters are speaking their thoughts that no one else can hear (asides or soliloquies) by using thought bubbles rather than speech balloons.

Of course, Wyeth would still be better off taking his students to see a live production of a Shakespeare play, or even watching one of the excellent versions on video, right? Perhaps. But graphic novel versions of the plays might allow students to more easily consider other layers of interpretation. Just as a theater or movie director makes choices about what themes of the play to emphasize, what time period to set the play in, and how to interpret the meaning and emphasis of the actors' lines, so do the writers and artists of a graphic novel version.

USING PICTURE/TEXT HYBRIDITY TO CREATE PERSONAL
CONNECTIONS AND INTERTEXTUAL CONNECTIONS

Another aspect of picture/text hybridity that may help Wyeth is the way that graphic novels provide additional ways for students to form both personal connections and intertextual connections to what they need.

Shakespeare can seem to students like it is old outdated material that doesn't relate to them. But by setting the plays in modern or futuristic locations, the Manga Shakespeare series, for example, may help students see Romeo and Juliet as two teenagers in love whose dysfunctional families oppose the relationship, or help them see Hamlet as the child of a stepfather who is a jerk and a mom who is oblivious to what her son is going through. Both of these scenarios are ones they can easily relate to. The image/text hybridity allows modern manga images to help students make that connection.

Intertextuality is the way that books, movies, and other media connect to one another. We can see intertextuality in such diverse examples as Mo Willems's picture books, Marvel movies, and the musical *Hamilton*. In each of these, references within the work connect to other works—Mo Willems's picture books connect to each other, Marvel movies connect to other Marvel movies and to decades of comic book lore, and the musical *Hamilton* connects not only to the biography of its title character but also to hip-hop albums and the current political landscape in the United States.

Intertextual references not only link the readert o a much broader conversation but also (much like inside jokes) make the reader feel that he or she is part of a community of those that know.

Graphic novels, like regular books, can, of course, make such references through text, as when a character uses a catch phrase or makes some other reference to a character from another book. And graphic novels can also make intertextual references through images alone, as in several graphic novels the setting for a late-night meeting for coffee bears a striking resemblance for Edward Hopper's painting Nighthawks.

Picture/text hybridity also allows graphic novels to use the intersection of picture and text to make intertextual references. Consider figure 6.1. The unsavory character who tells Jack to trust him on the very next page convinces jack to trade his mother's car keys for a collection of oddly packaged seeds. While the text (and the situation), along with Jack's name, immediately make a connection to the folk tale *Jack and the Beanstalk*, readers of Ben Hatke's other work will recognize both the words and manners of the unsavory character as Piper from the Zita series.

These sorts of connections strengthen student readers' connections not only to their works but also to the book they are reading, and quite possibly to strengthen the joy of reading itself.

USING PICTURE/TEXT HYBRIDITY TO PROVIDE
MULTIPLE PERSPECTIVES

When teachers think about multiple perspectives, they often think of English class (for example, telling a story from different points of view) or history class (considering an event from different political, cultural, or religious perspectives). In fact, though, one of the constants of education is that students learn better when they can approach a new concept or problem from multiple perspectives or with the aid of multiple examples or situations. When teaching math, science, physical education, or anything else, the more contexts in which a student can consider a new idea, the better.

The picture/text hybridity of graphic novels allows for the different perspectives in text that we are used to in regular prose (in graphic novels they are sometimes conveyed by giving different voices different-colored textboxes), but also allows for other perspectives to be expressed through the images in combinations with the words. One character might be asserting something and another character's face might be visible, showing a skeptical expression.

In history, for example, having multiple perspectives on an event can help the student-reader fully understand how different observers can see different aspects of the same event. The American civil rights struggle involved many different people and groups of people in many different ways. Ho Che Anderson's *King 1 and 2* is an unvarnished biography of Dr. Martin Luther King that provides insight into the thinking and strategizing of his top lieutenants and into his interactions with John and Robert Kennedy. Laird and Bey's *Still I Rise* puts the civil rights struggle in the context of over two centuries of African American history (and is told by two narrators—one who argues that African Americans are better off now than when they first came to America, and the other who argues the opposite).

PROVIDE A VISUALIZATION OF
ABSTRACT CONCEPTS OR PROCESSES

Teri, mentioned in the beginning of this chapter, is struggling with how to get her students familiar with a complicated series of concepts that link together to form a larger understanding—in this case how natural selection, genetic encoding, symbiosis of ecologies, paleontology, taxonomy, and epigenetics (and other concepts) combine to form evolutionary theory. That is a difficult agenda, since each of these concepts involves fairly complicated processes.

Sometimes teachers assess how well students have memorized the definitions associated with these concepts and processes—but what Teri is really hoping is that students will be able to see how all these working parts fit together to form the single dynamic system of evolutionary theory.

As was mentioned before, teachers often use blackboards, interactive whiteboards, visual aids, and hand gestures to get their points across. The range of ideas and examples, though, may require that Teri be either an award-winning illustrator or spend hours putting together a PowerPoint. She could extend her students' knowledge by requiring them to read a book on natural selection—but that book needs to convey the images and examples primarily through words. A graphic novel, in contrast, can incorporate words, images, charts, maps, photographs, and examples in the flow of the narrative.

For example, in Schultz, Cannon, and Cannon's *The Stuff of Life: A Graphic Guide to Genetics and DNA*, an alien who looks sort of like a starfish glued to the end of a sea cucumber is trying to explain to the leader of his people how human genetics works. In the far left panel in figure 6.2, the alien uses a projector to show closer and closer pictures of DNA. In the second panel he starts to explain how DNA works. The panels that follow show how DNA replicates itself, the panels combining realistic images of DNA with cartoon pictures of parts of cells and analogies of magnifying glasses to show how the parts of the DNA seek similar parts.

On this single two-page layout, we have an overall picture focusing in to a close-up, a likeable narrator telling the multiple analogies (including a safe and a magnifying glass), the personification of parts of the DNA, and multiple views from different perspectives to show the process. Throughout the images, the text works to provide a narrative explanation of what students are seeing.

Teri might use an approach like this in her classroom, combining a blackboard image with verbal explanation, but the graphic novel format does the same thing as Teri's class instruction and also allows students the possibility of jumping forward, reviewing, or looking back. This book will not necessarily replace Teri's textbook, nor will it reach all of her readers or solve all of the learning difficulties of her class. But clearly it is a useful tool to help students visualize the process in a variety of different ways.

Teri could choose to make the graphic novel available to those who are struggling with understanding, or to those who want to work ahead, or perhaps assign it to the entire class as an option for clarifying. Projecting excerpts onto a screen might also be valuable to give Teri some ready analogies to explain the process.

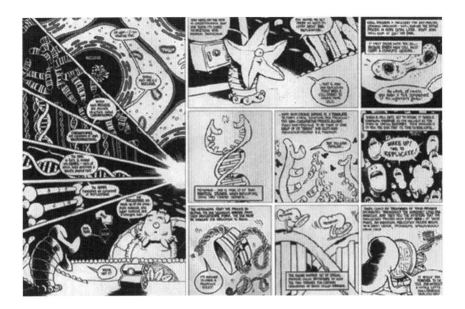

Figure 6.2.   Excerpt from "How the System Works—The Molecular Story," in *The Stuff of Life: A Graphic Guide to Genetics and DNA* by Mark Schultz, illustrated by Zander Cannon and Kevin Cannon. *Text © 2009 by Mark Schultz. Illustrations © 2009 by Zander Cannon and Kevin Cannon. Reprinted by permission of Hill and Wang, a division of Farrar, Straus and Giroux.*

CONCLUSION: PICTURE/TEXT HYBRIDITY IN GRAPHIC NOVELS CAN BE A USEFUL TOOL FOR TEACHING CONTENT

This chapter has included examples of how the picture/text hybridity in graphic novels can help convey content in a variety of ways: to build students' background knowledge, to extend teaching outside of lesson plans and classrooms, to provide additional depth and perspective beyond what textbooks offer, to create personal connections and intertextual connections; to provide multiple perspectives; and to provide a visualization of abstract concepts or processes.

While different disciplines, units, and lessons have different objectives and will require different methods, these six capabilities of graphic novels may serve as a guide as teachers determine how to use picture/text hybridity in their students' learning.

Chapter Seven

Disciplinary Inquiry Using Graphic Novels

As discussed in previous chapters, graphic novels can support a wide range of teaching and learning goals. One core goal of disciplinary literacy instruction is for students to engage in inquiry activities.

Inquiry is at the heart of disciplinary literacy (Manderino & Wickens, 2014). Deep disciplinary learning entails reading, writing, speaking, and listening while using disciplinary norms and conventions to investigate problems, interrogate representations, critique interpretations, create explanations, and discuss perspectives. In the classroom, teachers can create tasks and activities that make inquiry central to their lesson plans. These tasks are often driven by inquiry questions.

Graphic novels are well suited to this type of teaching for at least two important reasons. First, because graphic novels are generally regarded as a more casual medium, and because comic panels in our culture are mistakenly and exclusively associated with humor, students may find it easier to question their meaning, bias, approach, and content than textbooks or lengthy trade books, which often seem unassailably authoritative.

Second, graphic novels allow student-readers to not only interrogate the text but also the images. Some readers may have an easier time finding bias in depictions of characters or events, for example, than they would in text. In this way, graphic novels are useful tools when approaching inquiry questions.

Inquiry questions can vary in scope. They may be broad-based investigations that last several days or weeks. For example, a science inquiry unit may focus on how plate tectonics impact fault zones. A language arts unit might involve students asking questions about whether the Caldecott Honor–winning graphic novel *This One Summer* is more a story of hope or despair. In a history inquiry unit, students might gather first-person narratives of the civil rights movement and argue a conclusion based on what they find.

One way to frame inquiry is to first determine the type of inquiry you want students to engage in. Types of inquiry include:

1. *Open inquiry:* This is student-centered inquiry that is based on student-generated questions. For example, after an introduction to the effects that humans have on their environment, a science class might decide to analyze the quality of the runoff water in the stream behind the school.
2. *Guided inquiry:* This is inquiry where the teacher poses the questions that students investigate. For example, a history class considering the history of European colonization in Africa, Asia, and the Americas might be asked to select a colony to study, then divide into groups to read primary source documents and analyze the effects of colonization.
3. *Coupled inquiry:* The inquiry starts off as guided but moves to open inquiry. For example, after completing the history inquiry unit listed above, a teacher might ask students what more they want to know about other aspects or effects of colonization, then help them to frame an inquiry question to pursue.
4. *Structured inquiry:* This is inquiry that is very prescriptive and leads students to similar findings or shared understandings. A language arts teacher might have students pick two young adult novels, then work through a series of specific questions designed to help students consider those texts from a certain critical stance.

There is no one right way to engage in disciplinary inquiry. What is common to effective inquiry-based teaching is a change in the classroom from students passively acquiring content to using the techniques of a particular discipline to create content. Classroom-designed inquiry provides opportunities for disciplinary activities that are developmentally appropriate. Disciplinary inquiry that includes graphic novels deepens students' skills in navigating multiple representations for meaning making and meaning construction. Graphic novels support the types of text-based learning that are critical to building disciplinary literacies skills.

Many of the elements of the GRAPHIC framework are essential to planning for disciplinary inquiry. When using a disciplinary literacy approach, it is essential that teachers and their students take an inquiry stance toward the graphic novel they are working with. The role of graphic novels is not simply to provide an alternative representation to whatever other texts are in use, but to also provide a text that students can interrogate. As such, graphic novels can play multiple roles in the inquiry process.

THE ROLE OF TEXT IN INQUIRY

Multiple texts play an integral role in inquiry. Students need to be able to gather information from multiple sources; determine relevance, trustworthiness, and accuracy of information contained in texts; synthesize core ideas from texts; and communicate using disciplinary discourse in the form of discussion and writing. Graphic novels can play an important part of the text sets for disciplinary inquiry. Because inquiry is text driven, a wide variety of texts and text types can support disciplinary inquiry.

Graphic novels can serve a number of roles in the inquiry process. They may serve as the anchor text in the inquiry, a gateway activity to initiate inquiry (Lee, 2014), a text to provide a competing or alternative perspective, a text that provides an additional representation of the content, or one of several texts needed to come to an overarching understanding of the inquiry question.

Table 7.1 offers some examples of the role of graphic novels in disciplinary inquiry. The key in terms of instructional design is to select texts that engender disciplinary thinking and support content learning.

TEACHING DISCIPLINARY INQUIRY WITH GRAPHIC NOVELS

While graphic novels can be an essential resource, the affordances of graphic novels alone are not enough to lead students to disciplinary inquiry. The tasks designed with graphic novels are essential. The GRAPHIC framework works as an effective planning tool to design disciplinary inquiry with graph-

Table 7.1. Examples of Different Inquiry Roles across Disciplines

Discipline	Role of GN in Inquiry	Example GNs
ELA	Anchor text	*This One Summer; American Born Chinese; Pride of Baghdad*
Science	Extended representation	*The Stuff of Life: A Graphic Guide to Genetics and DNA; Primates: The Fearless Science of Jane Goodall, Dian Fossey, and Biruté Galdikas.*
Social Studies	Alternative perspective	*Still I Rise; A People's History of American Empire*
Math	Overall understanding of the concept	*Logicomix: An Epic Search for Truth; Who Killed Professor X?*

ic novels, but there are infinite ways to approach instruction using graphic novels. This section shares overarching ways to design disciplinary inquiry using graphic novels that capitalize on disciplinary learning goals.

SPARKING INQUIRY

Satchel Paige: Striking Out Jim Crow is a graphic novel that tells the story of Satchel Paige's career from the Negro Baseball Leagues onward. If a group of middle school students with very little prior knowledge about the Jim Crow era read this book, they would likely end that experience with a list of questions, perhaps including, Why are Jim Crow laws called that? How did those laws come to be? What made the Jim Crow laws go away? How come all-white teams were willing to play against African American teams? Why didn't people stand up against the Jim Crow laws?

Graphic novels are a great way to introduce a topic or get students interested in a topic that will be the focus of inquiry. But the questions they generate may not always be the ones that connect to the material teachers wish to study. How can we make choices so that graphic novels spark the inquiry questions we want them to spark?

The first step is to determine what the inquiry question is and which graphic novels might best support this inquiry. Some questions to ask may include: What prior knowledge do my students have on this topic? What level of interest do my students have on this topic? What experiences do my students have in this type of inquiry? When selecting a graphic novel to spark the inquiry process, also analyze the text for how it will support the inquiry. To analyze the text in relation to the task of introducing the inquiry, consider the checklist in table 7.2.

It is important that the graphic novel is not simply a hook to interest students in the content. While graphic novels will most likely engage students, a teacher must make the most of the graphic novel in the inquiry process. For example, graphic novels can challenge commonly held assumptions; provide an alternative perspective; pair with a text-based account of the same narrative, event, process, or concept; position the novel as a lever to evaluate subsequent texts; or introduce new or abstract concepts.

Regardless of purpose, if disciplinary learning objectives are clear, then disciplinary literacies can maximize texts for learning. Graphic novels open opportunities to build disciplinary literacies such as examining the beliefs and norms of the discipline, engaging in disciplinary habits of thinking and practice, or analyzing the text and language demands that are part of the way members of that discipline discuss, explain, and argue. Using graphic novels to spark inquiry not only invites students into the content but also invites

Table 7.2.   Graphic Novel Selection Evaluation Form

Name of Graphic Novel	*Number of Pages*
Will students read the whole text or excerpts?	If excerpts, what pages?

What key concepts will this graphic novel elicit for your inquiry?

What other texts connect with this graphic novel?

What will students do while reading this graphic novel?
*   Annotate
*   Participate in discussion groups
*   Summarize
*   Take notes
*   Other

them into a community of learners who can become insiders into the disciplines that the content resides.

SUPPORTING THE INQUIRY

Graphic novels may also serve as one of several texts in inquiry design. Excerpts, full graphic novels, and multiple graphic novels can all be a part of the overall text set used for disciplinary inquiry. It is important to determine the role graphic novels can play as supporting text in disciplinary inquiry. Any time multiple texts are used for inquiry, each text plays an important part. Texts can be complementary to each other, can be juxtaposed against the other text's perspective or argument, or they can stand alone to provide additional information that is not provided in the other texts.

Graphic novels are powerful texts to support inquiry because they can be used to reinforce key ideas, provide alternative perspectives and representations, and offer new, unique information compared to traditional text types. For example, in an inquiry unit about early Native American and European contact in North America, students might read a graphic novel such as George O'Connor's *Journey into Mohawk Country. Mohawk Country*, as was mentioned in an earlier chapter, that graphic novel uses the entire text of the journal of a Dutch explorer visiting the Mohawk settlements in what is now upstate New York and parts of Ontario to determine why the Mohawks seemed predisposed toward trading with the French more than the Dutch.

Read by itself, the journal is rather dull going. George O'Connor, however, uses what historians now know about the culture of the Mohawk people to argue that the explorer and his party were consistently committing a series of culturally inappropriate actions, such as feeding the tribal totem, a trapped black bear, whatever odd things they could find to see what the bear would eat. O'Connor makes these arguments solely through the images he draws, depicting the actions of the explorers—fleshing out what is left unsaid in the text. Thus in one book, student-readers can see both the original text and the interpretation, and then decide whether they buy into O'Connor's argument.

ANCHORING THE INQUIRY

Some graphic novels can serve as the single text that serves as the material around which an inquiry is constructed. Getz and Clarke's *Abina and the Important Men* is a great example of a text that could anchor an inquiry unit. *Abina* uses the graphic novel format to tell the true story of an Gold Coast woman who used the British legal system to sue the man who claimed her as a slave. After the graphic novel retelling of the story, the book includes a text chapter that gives the historical context of the story, the original court transcripts of the case, and the story of the historian who found out about the case.

There is enough material here for *Abina* to serve as the anchor of an inquiry unit. After reading the book, students could do additional research into the history of the Gold Coast and the history of human trafficking in the region, and even try to figure out what happened to Abina after the trial. It is not that an anchor text is the only text used in that inquiry, but rather that it is the text that is in the middle of the search.

A graphic novel can serve as an anchor text with other texts used in support of developing a deep understanding of the subject of the inquiry. If a graphic novel is used at the center of the inquiry, it is important to consider what other texts will support the reading of the graphic novel. Remember that disciplinary inquiry is predicated on the reading of multiple texts and representations. Even if a graphic novel is the primary text, analyzing other complementary texts is essential.

Using a graphic novel as the primary text is a great way to teach specific habits of thinking and practice in a discipline through the close reading of text. In the case of graphic novels, opportunities multiply because of the multimodal nature of graphic novels. Encourage students to read all three components of the graphic novel: text, image, and intersection of text and image.

Students should ask themselves why the creators of the graphic novel chose to depict characters/subjects, locations, and actions in the way they did. Why did the creators choose to juxtapose images against each other? Why did they select certain images to recur again and again? How do the images and text interact with each other?

When a graphic novel is the anchor of an inquiry, students should also have opportunities to create their own disciplinary explanations and interpretations based on their inquiry with the graphic novel. Disciplinary inquiry involves not merely consuming texts but also producing new ideas.

MOVING TOWARD DISCIPLINARY INQUIRY WITH GRAPHIC NOVELS

Graphic novels expand and deepen disciplinary learning. Used intentionally, they open possibilities for engagement in the disciplines beyond mere consumption of canonical narratives, explanations, and interpretations. Perhaps most promising is that they unveil ways to re-present and reimagine how to interpret literature, reconstruct the past, solve problems, and develop theories about scientific processes. Graphic novels serve as mentor texts that generate new representations of ideas that have been traditionally confined to printed word.

Chapter Eight

Critical Response

Assessment and graphic novels may not necessarily come to mind as obvious pairings, but that may be more as a result of how to think of assessment than any natural antipathy between the two. In assessment, it is important to begin with an understanding of what one is assessing and why, before moving on to things like appropriate format.

With the GRAPHIC framework, the goals of teaching, along with the resources, approaches, appreciation for the picture/text hybridity, as well as methods of inquiry are all up front, before ending with the "C" of "critical response." The reframing of general assessment as critical response underscores the broader aspects of understanding assessments in conjunction with graphic novels.

Too often our view of assessment only encompasses summative assessments, which ignores the multitude of other ways in which teachers can assess or have students respond to texts before, during, and after instruction. This chapter is named "Critical Response" in order to invoke the many ways in which graphic novels can be used to elicit student responses, and how that information can be used for both formative and summative purposes, as well as demonstrate broader reader responses and processes.

Paralleling chapters 4 and 5, this chapter may help you to view assessment with graphic novels through two lenses: (1) assessment of disciplinary habits of thinking and practice and (2) assessment of disciplinary content. By unpacking how students understand and interpret information conveyed in graphic novels, whether through critical responses of text—such as literary or visual analysis—or through their own original responses and syntheses, teachers can better understand their grasp of disciplinary skills and content.

Furthermore, having inhabited a liminal space historically, graphic novels are uniquely situated to include and address marginalized experiences that push at more critical understandings of a discipline. Graphic novels can often offer an underrepresented or alternative view on a topic, undergirding possibilities for discussions around critical issues and themes. Mastery of a discipline, even an elementary, developing mastery, is not just about bland retention of facts and figures but understanding that disciplines are fraught with conflicts and contradictions. This requires active engagement and a critical understanding of context, content, and characters.

Because graphic novels can either stand alone in teaching disciplinary content and skills and/or be used in conjunction with teaching and supplementing traditional texts, teachers should be clear going *into* their teaching about several elements. It is important to know what the purpose in teaching with the graphic novel is, what students should take away from the lesson/unit, and how to assess student learning at the end of the lesson/unit. Not having a clear focus through the process can create stumbling blocks for teachers in the assessment process.

In teaching with graphic novels, objectives may align with disciplinary, critical literacy, or social justice–oriented goals. As discussed previously, graphic novels can help teachers relay disciplinary content and habits of thinking and practice. Aligning assessments or critical responses with intended goals is important in accurately determining instructional success. As has been demonstrated in the last several chapters, graphic novels offer a wide variety of ways in which to teach students. However, without having students critically respond to their learning, teachers cannot truly know how effective their teaching was.

While graphic novels can be a motivating way to engage students, they can also help to convey and interpret dense and difficult material in a more accessible manner. This can obviously be the case when reading a graphic adaptation of Shakespeare or *Beowulf*. However, it can also aid students' abilities to practice discipline-specific practices, like corroborating or understanding context.

GRAPHIC NOVELS AS PRIMARY, COMPLEMENTARY, OR SUPPLEMENTARY TEXTS

The manner in which the graphic novel is used in teaching will drive the types and substance of assessments deployed. In delivering content, teachers may choose to use graphic novels as three different text types:

Primary

* As the anchor text

Complementary

- As a competing or alternative perspective
- As additional representation of content

Supplementary

- As a gateway activity to initiate or close a lesson/unit
- As ancillary support materials

When teachers first determine the ways in which the graphic novels will be used—as primary, complementary, or supplementary texts—this should also help determine some of the content and methods in which they will teach it. For example, if an English teacher is teaching a graphic adaptation of *Macbeth*, that teacher will need to decide which version he or she will use, assessing the value of each in terms of

- Fidelity to original text
- Inclusion and exclusion of details of the original text
- Authenticity of representation
- Utility for teaching literary devices
- Other concerns

Depending on which text the teacher uses and whether he or she uses it as the primary or complementary text, there will be certain affordances or constraints placed upon the teacher's ability to assess the students.

Again, depending on the goal and approaches of teaching with the graphic novel, there are different ways teachers can ask students to critically respond to their learning. If the graphic novel is being used as the primary text, typical reader responses or learning logs might be recommended to help students track their learning.

Because of the intense amount of information the visual format includes beyond just plain text, students may need to be taught how to read graphic novels carefully and how to track or make note of their learning. For example, annotating with sticky notes while reading may be particularly beneficial here in place of the traditional textual marginal annotations—even as some of those annotations will be made in reference to the visual aspects and not just the print.

Students may also need to be guided to understand how characters might be depicted visually and how this may reveal information about their nature, or to create personal glossaries when historical figures and ideas become too cumbersome to simply remember. However, as we have said before, the informal nature in which students may view graphic novels—as more approachable or childish—may allow for them to be more critical in their responses to text than traditional texts.

For example, students may be inclined to disagree with an artist's depiction of a character or the ways in which the character is portrayed. While they might not feel confident to question a written description of the character—appearing as it does in authoritative black-and-white text—because the drawn image of the character adds another layer of interpretation, the students may have an easier time engaging in critical response to the visual images than traditional texts.

If the graphic novel is being used as a complementary or supplementary text, it will be important for teachers to have taught students how to compare and work from multiple texts. Depending on whether the graphic novel is being used as another perspective or a reinforcement of learning, it is important that students know how to read and process multiple texts. Within disciplinary practices, this may include things like authorial intent and qualification, corroboration of sources or perspectives, and synthesis across the various sources.

The following scenario explores how using graphic novels as primary, complementary, or supplementary texts might impact how a teacher asks students to respond to them critically. If the graphic adaptation updates and modifies the story and language of Shakespeare's *Macbeth*, the teacher may not be able to ask students to do explicit textual analysis of Shakespearean language use. If the teacher is using this updated adaptation as an anchor text, the teacher would assess more plot-based or character-based content rather than the language itself. Additionally, if the teacher is concerned about students learning certain literary devices like foreshadowing or tone, students may need to be taught how to "read" or decipher the images and relay their understanding of that visual interpretation in an assessment.

On the other hand, if this adaptation was more of a plot reinforcement *alongside* the original text, students may be freed up to grapple more with the language and intricacies of Shakespearean language instead of basic plot structure. In that case, the adaptation helps the students grasp the story, but the teacher could still assess students' understanding of Shakespearean language based on their reading of the original text and not the graphic adaptation.

This would also allow room to explore potential critical responses to Shakespeare, for example, examining his treatment of women; discussing race, class, and power; or even doing comparative textual analysis of the graphic novel's fidelity to Shakespeare's essence.

The teacher may prefer to use an abridged graphic adaptation that still remains relatively close to the original Shakespearean language. In this case, using a graphic adaptation as the anchor text, the teacher can assess for content (plot and language) alongside visual components and literary devices. Teachers may also use a variety of graphic adaptations and texts to teach the disciplinary skill of interpretation. This would allow them to assess how students understand and evaluate interpretations of text, as well as how they demonstrate analysis and comparison skills.

CRITICAL RESPONSE

Because of the relatively recent phenomenon of incorporating graphic novels into the classroom, teachers have lagged in determining how best to have students critically respond in meaningful ways to the picture/text hybridity we've discussed previously. In other words, when images and text are inextricably intertwined, how does one determine in what manner to assess student understanding? What gets foregrounded?

Understandably, some educators have moved toward having students create their own graphic responses as a form of assessment. While this has a certain relevancy, it still doesn't necessarily get at the heart of understanding the hybrid format and meaning-making affordances of graphic novels. It more likely assesses student understanding of the graphic novel format, rather than the material at hand.

Furthermore, it can also penalize students who are not artistically inclined. This oversimplification of the picture/text hybridity diminishes the complexity of the image and the opportunities for critical engagement. Students analyzing the picture/text hybridity have more opportunities to consider everything from how individuals or situations are portrayed to issues of power and representation on a page.

What is, in some ways, a glorified "sketch-to-stretch" strategy doesn't teach or deeply assess student understanding of content or concepts. The remainder of the chapter will explore the various ways in which graphic novels can engage better opportunities for critical response before, during, and after lessons or units.

DISCIPLINARY CONTENT

Elementary teachers are quite familiar with using graphics or illustrations to help elicit student prior knowledge and build schema before a reading. Whether doing a "picture walk" for a book or having extensive conversations about the cover before reading, elementary students are primed more often about using illustrations to make predictions, build schema, and even check comprehension than the typical secondary student.

Secondary teachers can take a cue and select specific panels or pages to introduce the graphic novel and how to read it (if it's a new form for them), as well as discussing what may happen in the text before reading. Because of the intensity of text and illustration on one single page with its many panels, secondary teachers may also consider spending some time discussing a few select pages to help introduce characters, setting, and practice analysis of the illustrations for clues about the reading. Graphic novels can be a great way to help engage readers in material before fully embarking on a new unit.

Another unique way to have students critically respond to graphic novels before reading—regardless of whether they are being used as primary, complementary, or supplementary texts—is to provide several panels without text to elicit student prior knowledge or help prime their schema and text-reading skills.

When students are asked to fill in what may be happening or what they notice about the illustrations, they are being offered opportunities to be more metacognitive and deliberate in their reading and understandings. "Priming" student interest and awareness mirrors the kinds of self-reflection experts in their disciplines engage in before tackling a text. It can also help set a purpose for reading, as individuals look to answer questions, fill in gaps in understanding, or corroborate previous understanding.

Interestingly, despite popular misconceptions that graphic novels may be watered-down versions of "real" writing, many graphic novels have higher levels of vocabulary than typical grade-level material. Part of the reason for this is the sheer lack of space in a panel, which drives the need for the best, most appropriate and concise writing. In this manner, students may be exposed to more high-level vocabulary and have more context clues from which to make meaning.

This kind of multimodal meaning making is also drawn upon heavily within the disciplines, as readers are expected to read and understand figures, pictures, and tables. In the example that follows, a page from the graphic novel *Feynman*, there are both words and concepts that are sophisticated and arguably difficult to understand.

In the graphic novel page shown in figure 8.1, Feynman uses words and terms such as "QED," "synthesis," "phenomena," "magnetism," "wave theory," "infrared," "ultraviolet," and so on. To support the reader's understanding, the book also provides Feynman's facial expressions, guest appearances by Sir Isaac Newton and James Clark Maxwell, and an image of a pit viper and a bee on either end of the light wave spectrum. Because graphic novel layouts require space for the images, the words appear in smaller groups, allowing readers to digest them in smaller portions. Yet when you read the page, the concepts and vocabulary are neither easy nor watered down in any way.

Graphic novels are rarely monolithic in any way—which is to say you can certainly find graphic novels out there with overly simplified or watered-down concepts and vocabulary, just as you can find conventional books that take a similar approach. But as the example illustrates, even though graphic novels have supports built in that can increase the supports and context clues

Figure 8.1. From *Feynman* © 2011 by Jim Ottaviani. Illustrations © 2011 by Leland Myrick. *Reprinted by permission of First Second, an imprint of Roaring Brook Press, a division of Holtzbrinck Publishing Holdings Limited Partnership. All rights reserved.*

for the readers, there is nothing in the format that requires or even encourages simplifying ideas or vocabulary.

Using some of the panels with high-level vocabulary to teach the words before asking students to read a particular graphic novel can be an excellent way to teach both graphic novel reading skills and to prime students' prior knowledge. Having students respond in writing or verbally about how they read graphic novel texts can help you better understand how students are thinking about texts *before* reading. Additionally, having students respond *during* reading and reflecting on their understanding of newly encountered words also provides you with information about how students are navigating the material and their strategies in doing so.

When using graphic novels as a complementary or supplementary text, teachers can also use shorter excerpts of a graphic novel to introduce concepts or skills crucial to understanding the primary text(s). For example, teachers can use one of the "uncelebrated narratives" of Gill's *Strange Fruit* before beginning a text or unit on African American heroes or the civil rights movement to help students start thinking critically about the themes of everyday heroism or the courage needed to overcome the institutionalized racism of various time periods.

The highly visual element of graphic novels, and the picture/text hybridity of which we've spoken, lend themselves to help students think about major issues and ideas of texts. Having students respond through writing or discussion with the graphic novel excerpt allows them an entry point to engage in the potentially denser material of the primary text.

Teachers can work with graphic novel excerpts to teach and practice literary elements, such as tone or characterization, which lend themselves particularly well to the visual element. Graphic novels provide an opportunity to support predominantly visual learners (and stretch those whose visual learning is still developing) before transitioning to moving on to print-only text. The visual features can help readers more actively engage in the process of comprehending texts and literary devices like metaphor, symbolism, point of view, intertextuality, narrative structure, and inference.

For example, a graphic novel may provide visual cues to more abstract textual shifts, like change in narration, by outlining the text in different colors or changing the font. They may show flashbacks in a different textbox or highlight inner thought using different visual clues, all features that help engage students' understanding. By eliciting students' critical responses with graphic texts, teachers can help build students' skill sets to apply toward print-only texts.

Having students engage the same critical skills with two different formats also activates the higher-level thinking involved in transfer (applying learned skills to new situations). All of these critical responses can provide important clues for teachers on the information and skills students are bringing to a text or unit.

Finally, because a variety of graphic novels can offer the possibilities for expressing historically marginalized perspectives, using such texts before a unit with more traditional literature can provide a more nuanced and contextualized understanding of the material. This may be particularly important with uses of textbooks that may obfuscate or diminish the contributions of people of color, women, or other underrepresented populations.

DISCIPLINARY HABITS OF THINKING AND PRACTICE

It is helpful to think of assessment with graphic novels more in terms of critical response and as both summative *and* formative. Asking students to engage in thinking about their learning as they work through texts is important. Whether monitoring for comprehension or demonstrating how they wrestle with making connections, having students critically engage with their learning both highlights difficulties in comprehension and reinforces successful learning.

Depending on how the graphic novels are being used, as primary, complementary, or supplementary texts, students can track their comprehension using typical literacy strategies like text annotation and reading logs. Asking students to engage in such reflective behavior mirrors the kinds of knowledge tracking scientists engage in through tasks like a lab notebook.

However, the visual element within the graphic novel allows for some more interesting opportunities to respond. In typical print-only textual annotation, students may note difficult concepts or terms, ask questions about the text, or make connections to other texts. With the inclusion of the visual element, though, there are more obvious opportunities to critique author/ illustrator choice in representation and bias, as well as engaging in more fine-grained analysis of context.

The picture/text hybridity also creates opportunities for students to evaluate text and image side by side to determine whether they work together to create a harmonious meaning or whether they create a contrast in meaning that must be further analyzed. For example, consider the page from *Journey into Mohawk Country* shown in figure 8.2. You recall, this is the graphic novel with the text of the Dutch explorer's diary and George O'Connor's images to fill in imagined details. You might have students read this page then ask how the images and text work together.

Clearly the images do not merely echo the text but provide a bit of irony that makes us question the reliability of the narrator. For example, at the top of the page where the journal states that the Mohawks say they want to be friends, their facial expressions do not fit with the way a contemporary reader

Figure 8.2.   From *Journey into Mohawk Country* © 2006 by George O'Connor. *Reprinted by permission of First Second, an imprint of Roaring Brook Press, a division of Holtzbrinck Publishing Holdings Limited Partnership. All rights reserved.*

would expect such a statement. When Harmen looks up from playing dice at the imposing figures above him and says that he told the Mohawk men that they were not afraid, there is something in his expression that causes readers to think he is mostly trying to reassure himself.

In the final panel, the text and image support each other without irony or sarcasm, but the imposing nature of Harmen and his two companions in a dark room with a council of twenty-four men continues the impression from previous panels that the Dutch explorers are in over their heads. While requiring some thought, this sort of analysis is within the capabilities of high school English students.

This analysis of meaning as reinforcing or contradicting previous understanding can also be applied when using graphic novels alongside print-only texts. Students can respond via discussion or writing to similarities and differences they see between texts, looking at issues of authorial choice, representation, perspectives, and critically analyzing for accuracy. Film adaptations of literature are one example of how this occurs already.

One popular point of contention in film adaptations is in casting—whether the choice of an actor was appropriate or accurate. Parallel discussions of interpretation can be had in examining graphic adaptations of texts, particularly if the language has been adapted as well. Students will have to more closely examine characterization and language to better understand how effective or accurate a graphic adaptation may be (and perhaps to question the choices the artist made in depicting certain characters in that particular way).

Similarly, used within a text set with other materials, students would have the opportunity to demonstrate greater understanding in evaluating source material, corroborating ideas, or questioning the materials. By confronting students with multiple texts in different genres or formats, students must demonstrate how they puzzle out valuing meanings of one text over another, reflecting on differences, or constructing their understanding on a topic.

This multiplicity of possibilities lends itself toward opportunities for disciplinary and interdisciplinary learning. How can reading a graphic novel about the personal toll of cancer on a family help science students understand the moral and ethical dilemmas of scientific advancements? How can asking students to read multiple versions of the same story and determining their veracity or bias, or synthesizing their own unique meaning sharpen their critical skills?

In this age of polarizing headlines, overly rigid perspectives, and a world increasingly fraught with us-versus-them mentality, perhaps the power of using graphic novels to teach empathy and promote multiple perspectives cannot be oversold. Graphic novels can help provide firsthand insights into the experiences of others and provide opportunities to view how others negotiate these fraught and contested spaces. By asking students to document their learning as they wrestle with and question these perspectives, students are also being asked to practice how to engage critically with the world.

BECAUSE YOU CAN'T RESIST

From the underground zine to web comics, the marriage of picture and text in panels has a long and storied history of subversion. While not all graphic novels convey the experiences or perspectives of the marginalized or disenfranchised, that is a part of their history and an ongoing tradition. As noted in previous chapters, many graphic novels provide alternate perspectives, multifaceted and nuanced story lines, and complex contexts.

Even if students don't fully grasp all of the allusions or references in a graphic novel, graphic novels' ability to engage readers may further motivate them to research or reflect further upon things they did not understand. The graphic novel series *Lumberjanes* by Noelle Stevenson, Shannon Watters, and Brooke A. Allen is rife with rich and varied references to feminist ideas and icons. Students can read criticism published in journals that delineate these references.

Asking students to reflect on their experiences grappling with, exploring, and integrating such new knowledge from graphic novels—even if it is a rejection of the information presented—pushes them to practice academic skills of reflection and justification of ideas. Too often, students view learning as a passive activity, a consumption of ideas meant to be regurgitated en masse on the next exam. Having to analyze and synthesize multiple or contradicting perspectives requires a more actively engaged student. Even something as simple as asking students to side with whether a graphic novelist depicted an incident or concept accurately requires students to critically grapple with their understanding.

Students responding via their own comic interpretations to graphic novels or general learning can provide great learning opportunities for students to respond critically. However, many graphic novels are not written *and* illustrated by the same individual, and it is a time- and resource-intensive process. In order to make such comic critical responses a rich learning opportunity, it is important to engage in discussions about what the creation of comics or graphic novels looks like and understand their affordances and limitations.

Think of it this way: just because one knows how to *read* a novel does not necessarily mean one knows how to *write* one, or to write a *good* one, as any editor can tell you. Yet there seems to be a siren call for teachers to have students create graphic responses. If considering this, please make sure to discuss with students how comics work (there are several online resources to help, or consider using Scott McCloud's now classic *Understanding Comics*) and consider having students work in groups to collaboratively draw and write them.

Teachers should have a firm grasp of their objectives in teaching and what they are hoping to assess. Make sure to assess students' learning, not students' artistry (unless teaching an art class). Better still, give students a variety of ways to respond critically to what they have read, and assess their ability to respond critically, whether through artistic means or in other ways.

Chapter Nine

Themes, Interdisciplinary Instruction, and Graphic Novels

One of the things that distinguish high school and middle school from the elementary grades is the way instruction is broken up into separate disciplines. Having students learn different ways of disciplinary thinking allows them to bring a broad range of problem-solving skills to any situation. But at the same time, dividing knowledge into discrete boxes can cause students to forget that almost all knowledge, all problems, and all solutions are connected.

At this point in the history of graphic novels, the publishing industry has yet to figure out how to classify graphic novels by genre, target audience, and reading demographic. Most graphic novels are not yet for specific age groups or targeted for certain academic disciplines. This makes them an excellent resource for interdisciplinary units, which try to get at the areas of knowledge that fall between the cracks of the academic categories.

This chapter will consider ways that graphic novels can lead students to see thematic connections that flow between different disciplines.

GOALS

Why bother with having students study interdisciplinary themes? The many reasons tend to fall into these three categories:

1. Interdisciplinary themes can bridge interest and engagement for students from one discipline to another.
2. Interdisciplinary themes allow students to practice transferring skills and understandings from one discipline to another.

3. Interdisciplinary units provide opportunities to practice using distributed knowledge in problem solving.

This chapter will consider each of these larger goals in turn and look at how to embed smaller content- and skill-based goals within them.

One of the most difficult parts of teaching high school and middle school is dealing with students who are not interested in the subject matter being taught. Often such students are willing to pour passion and endless amounts of effort and time into what interests them outside of school but seem unwilling to contribute even a fraction of such time to a subject they perceive as being irrelevant. Interdisciplinary study can be a way to get your students to see that the skills and interests they already have can apply to academic situations as well. For example, imagine two high school students, Kate and Frances.

Kate's favorite subject is history. She likes learning why things have happened in the past and is passionate about social justice issues in the present. She has participated in protests in the city near where she lives and writes about justice issues in her blog, which has been linked to twice by a national blog that focuses on getting kids involved in politics. Her least favorite class is physical education. It isn't that she has no interest in being healthy, she just doesn't see the point in sports and organized games.

Frances loves to run. She is on the volleyball team and the track team, has run several 10K races, and is training to run her first half marathon. She does well in math and science but doesn't much like history. She thinks of history as a collection of boring dates and uninteresting passages about treaties and economic influences that are not relevant to her life, all wrapped up in a huge textbook.

A thematic unit about the impact African Americans in sports have had on history might give Kate the opportunity to discover how sports have had an impact on social justice issues. She can read about Jackie Robinson's debut as the first African American baseball player. She can learn about his remarkably difficult journey of ill treatment and abuse and restraint, as well as his ultimately triumphant career that shattered the color barrier and changed the way many people thought about African American athletes. This is not to say that PE will become Kate's new favorite class, but she might approach it with a different attitude.

The transfer of interest in an interdisciplinary unit can work both ways. Frances may learn about Jesse Owens and the 1936 Berlin Olympics. and discover that running, which she considers purely recreational, had an important role in disrupting Adolph Hitler's attempt to use the Olympics to make a political statement about Nazi superiority. Like Kate, Frances may not suddenly become the most enthusiastic history student in the room, but she may make some connections that let her start to see the value in studying it.

A second overall goal for interdisciplinary thematic units is to help students see how that which they learn in one particular discipline can transfer to another discipline. This can also be a matter of skills or concepts transferring. For example, one of the authors recalls taking a graphic design course in college at the same time he was taking a creative writing class. One of the ways of organizing elements on a page from the graphic design course was to arrange similar images in a grid, but then introduce an anomalous element: for example, if there is a grid of pictures of cows and then the artist removes one cow, replacing it with a picture of George Washington, people will be naturally drawn to the thing that doesn't belong.

It is exciting when one realizes this approach could be used for constructing a short story as well. An unexpected character or narrative twist serves the same function by breaking up an existing predictable pattern in the story much like George Washington's image did in the grid. Those connections are always stronger when it is the student who discovers them.

A different but related type of transfer falls under the heading of intertextuality. You might remember that intertextuality is a term that refers to the interconnectedness of texts. This could include moments in school when students realize that their history text is mentioning how Pablo Picasso's painting *Guernica*, which they were analyzing in art class the hour before, captured the horror of the Spanish Civil War; when students in English class catch a reference to *Hamlet* in a young adult novel; or when students watching the latest movie reboot of Superman catch a reference to something that happened in an important run of the comic book.

Intertextuality only works if students have prior knowledge of other works, and so it has limited capacity to spark student interest in a new area for them. Nonetheless, it can be a powerful motivating force. The feeling that readers get when they discover an intertextual reference is a good one. It is a bit like when someone in a group of friends tells an inside joke. When the entire group laughs at that joke, they share the experience and often feel a sense of belonging or bonding.

James Gee (2014) refers to affinity groups—people who share an interest or passion. Every time students catch an intertextual reference, they feel as though they are part of a special group. High school discipline-area teachers can use this to increase the students' identities as athletes, future English majors, budding scientists, people who understand math, and so on. Thus, intertextuality can deepen a student's commitment to a particular academic discipline.

Interdisciplinary units can also provide opportunities for students to practice using distributed knowledge in problem solving. Teachers often hear about the importance of having students work in a group, though they might not think about the reason for engaging in this practice. In fact, working in teams allows people to make the most of distributed knowledge.

Think of all the specialized knowledge it takes for someone to be able to board an airplane and fly to another part of the world. A team of mechanics, including experts in jet engines, electrical systems, hydraulics, controls, aerodynamics, and structural integrity, check over the plane. The pilot, copilot, and navigator, along with those in the control tower, figure out the best course to follow. Flight attendants and the gate crew make sure the passengers are seated quickly and comfortably. The baggage crew makes sure the luggage travels to the passengers' destination. The grounds crew fuels and provisions the plane and guides it in and out of the gate.

It would be practically impossible for all of these people to learn all of this information, but provided they communicate, they form a network of distributed knowledge. Together, they can solve problems, improve systems, and accomplish the amazing task of transporting hundreds of people safely through the air from one city to another. The lives of those passengers are quite literally dependent on the ability of those teams to communicate with each other effectively.

A well-constructed interdisciplinary unit can, in a similar way, make the most of students' different experiences, knowledge, interests, and expertise. For example, a unit that combines topics from history and science to produce a culminating documentary film using the talents of artists, writers, organizers, and performers is a remarkable example of distributed intelligence.

But what role can graphic novels play in all this? Well, while some graphic novels are written to be curricular textbooks for specific disciplines, most of them are more like trade books. Imagine the nonfiction section of a bookstore or a library. There you will find many books about many subjects—but most of them will transcend disciplinary boundaries. There are a great many graphic novels that do the same.

Because graphic novels are multimodal, they automatically incorporate elements of art, writing, and drama, and so have built-in connections to other disciplines. But perhaps the best way to understand how graphic novels can support interdisciplinary units is to look at some specific examples.

RESOURCES

Choosing resources for an interdisciplinary unit can be a bit different from choosing resources for a regular unit within your discipline. The primary difference is that an interdisciplinary unit usually has a bit more flexibility than a regular unit, partly to allow for a greater range of discovery as both students and teachers dig into the subject.

When working with disciplinary units, it is sometimes helpful to think of two different types of texts: anchor texts and supporting texts. Anchor texts are those that serve to introduce the topic, issue, or main idea. Graphic novels are sometimes a good choice for anchor texts because the combination of text and image often holds potential for evoking an emotional response.

Interdisciplinary units on social justice issues, for example, might use an anchor text like Gene Yang's *American Born Chinese* to begin a discussion about stereotypes. Similarly, John Lewis's *March* series might be a good way to introduce a unit on the civil rights movement and its effects on our contemporary world. Brooke Gladstone's *The Influencing Machine* would be an excellent anchor text for a unit on discernment of media and advertising.

Supporting texts are those texts available in a classroom library or on reserve at the school library because the teacher thinks students might need to turn to them, though that teacher also recognizes that student research may go in a different direction. Here, too, graphic novels have much to offer. For example, in the unit on the civil rights movement, one team of students might choose to concentrate on the impact of national sports on the fight for civil rights. Those students might choose to look at Wilfred Santiago's *21: The Story of Roberto Clemente* or James Sturm and Rich Tommaso's *Satchel Paige: Striking Out Jim Crow.*

Other student teams might decide to go in a different direction and instead look at other topics related to civil rights. Supporting texts for different directions that students might decide to focus on could include Toufic El Rassi's *Arab in America* as well as other graphic novels about the civil rights movement that were mentioned earlier in this book.

Similarly, for a unit on the sixties, teachers might want to have Arne Bellstorf's *Baby's in Black: Astrid Kirchherr, Stuart Sutcliffe, and the Beatles* handy for any students interested in the music of the sixties, but they might also want to keep Gene Yang's *Boxers* and *Saints* handy. This is not because it is about America during the sixties (it isn't—it is about China during the Boxer Rebellion)—but because Yang's overall theme that war is futile might be a way for students to connect to the frustration about the Vietnam War.

Of course, many other graphic novels deal with the sixties, including Buhle, Pekar, and Piskor's *The Beats: A Graphic History* and Dwight Jon Zimmerman and Wayne Vansant's *The Vietnam War: A Graphic History.*

When preparing an interdisciplinary unit, start with the anchor texts. Including at least one graphic novel will help connect the unit with multimodal learners. Reviews, recommendations, and award winners are good places to start, but as with regular books, reading the actual text is crucial for teachers as they are planning the unit. When determining readability, remember to pay attention not only to the word vocabulary, but the difficulty of interpreting images and panel shifts.

With interdisciplinary studies, remember to consider those elements of both word and image vocabularies that are particular to the component disciplines. Image vocabulary in this case might refer to iconic images (e.g., the radioactive symbol in physics), photographs that carry added meaning (e.g., the image of the marines on Iwo Jima), charts that are instantly recognizable to those in the field (e.g., the periodic table of the elements) and any other images needed to clarify concepts for students.

Be sure to check the back pages of the graphic novels you are investigating. Some graphic novels, like George O'Connor's series on Greek mythology, will provide notes in the back explaining the significance of particular visual elements. Rest assured, students will also point out some of these that teachers might not have noticed themselves.

APPROACHES

When thinking about interdisciplinary units, it is easy to forget that disciplinary discourses are still happening. It isn't so much that interdisciplinary work means we avoid the disciplines. It is more like bringing together several experts in different fields and asking them to work together on the same problem. At first they will need to work out what different languages they are speaking (e.g., archaeologists and paleontologists mean different things when they speak of layers—or even time). And who are the experts in this situation? The teacher, the students, and the texts—they all need to talk to each other.

That conversation becomes more complex, interesting, and powerful when graphic novels come into the mix. In the case of an interdisciplinary conversation, students need to remember that disciplinary discourse is carried in the words, in the images, and in the connection between the two. So this means that the images in a history graphic novel may be using a different pictorial language than the ones in a math graphic novel.

This would be a good topic for a discussion with students early on in an interdisciplinary unit. Ask them how the word language is different in books representing different disciplines, but also ask them about the visual language differences. Then, when they are warmed up, ask if they notice any difference in different disciplinary graphic novels in terms of the way the image and text combinations work. See if they can find specific examples.

It is also possible that the overlap between two disciplines may require coining some new words to describe text or image. Don't shy away from doing so. New language comes with the territory when exploring.

PICTURE/TEXT HYBRIDITY

It is important when using graphic novels in instruction to remind students to look at the words, the images, and the intersections of the words and images. While interdisciplinary work can take students into areas where they have a lot of prior knowledge and feel comfortable, it can also take them into new disciplines or subdisciplines. Graphic novels can be helpful for students to find their way into new knowledge, but students may also need to be reminded that new knowledge takes time to fully grasp.

There is a difference between how students read a narrative text and how they read an expository text. In reading a graphic novel that is primarily a story, students are first looking for visual elements that distinguish characters and settings, facial expressions that indicate emotion, and elements that move the plot forward. Of course, they are looking for many other aspects as well including interesting voices, historical facts, image details, and countless others, but it is the story elements—plot, character, and voice—that drive the movement of the book.

Expository graphic novels, on the other hand, though they may incorporate narrative structures from time to time, tend to be organized thematically or by processes, depending on what they are explaining. Once again, the discipline may determine the organization of the book. As we mentioned earlier, Schultz, Cannon, and Cannon's *The Stuff of Life* uses a narrative—a somewhat humorous one with an alien scientist trying to explain human life to his pompous leader—to provide an overall structure, and that leader's questions direct the general flow of the book, but because it is a science book, there is a lot of explanation about how biological processes work.

Joe Sacco's *Safe Area Gorazde*, a reporter's account of the Bosnian War, is organized chronologically, like many history books, but also looks at different first-person accounts and verifies or questions the veracity of those accounts. Math-based graphic novels can be organized in different ways, but almost always have a problem-solving component to their organization.

Whether reading narrative or expository graphic novels it is wise for readers to stop after a page or two and consider how the book is organized.

INQUIRY

Much has already been written about interdisciplinary instruction and inquiry and since there is not space enough to summarize all of that literature here, this chapter will restrict itself to some recommendations for using graphic novels in ways that promote interdisciplinary inquiry.

1. Show students the basics of how to read a graphic novel. Explain what order to read the panels in; how to read expressions and body positioning; how to read mood; how to understand the difference between speech bubbles, thought bubbles, and narration boxes; and then discuss any basic questions they might have. This basic level of learning

will give them the vocabulary they will need to discuss what they read in relation to what they want to find out and what they are finding out.

2. Model how to read graphic novels. If this is the first time some students have used graphic novels, it would help to give them some examples of how to use them. Project the first few pages (using a document camera or scanning a couple of pages of the graphic novel and showing them using a classroom projector). If that is not an option, a class set of graphic novels would help. If that isn't possible, teachers could also photocopy the first few pages. Teachers could then track with a finger and model what they are looking for, what they are noticing, and especially what critical questions they are asking as they read.

3. Discuss what the habits of thinking within each discipline can bring to interdisciplinary inquiry. Of course, it would be helpful if students have already had some instruction about different disciplines and how they work, but even without this, it is possible to have a class discussion about what the goals and techniques of each discipline are, and how to use them. For example, in an interdisciplinary unit looking at the role of photojournalism in war, and combining the disciplines of history, art, and English, a class might note that history evaluates different accounts of events to construct a combined narrative of what happened; art allows for careful visual analysis; and English examines purpose and interprets voice and language. In fact, the class might be able to make a longer list than this example for each discipline.

4. Discuss how graphic novels might interact with each of those disciplinary aspects. During the photojournalism unit, students might discover Morvan, Trefouel, and Bertail's *Omaha Beach on D-day*. This book combines a graphic novel format with photos and regular text to tell the story of photographer Robert Capa, the only photojournalist to go ashore with the first wave of Allied troops on D-day in World War II.

5. After reading the book, there is much students might observe about the format. The story includes Robert Capa's perspective on the invasion; and the accounts of Huston Riley who was in one of Capa's photographs, and John Morris who was the London head of photography of *Life* magazine. The story of the photographs is told in graphic novel format, but the book includes the photographs themselves, which allows for visual analysis. The graphic novel narrative also uses the narration boxes to include Robert Capa's voice, but also uses speech balloons to include other voices. This gives students the chance to learn not only about the topic of their interdisciplinary study, but also to think critically about the way they are learning and understanding that knowledge—a valuable way to learn critical thinking.

6. Once students know how to use graphic novels, encourage them to select, read, evaluate, and use graphic novels as part of their own projects. Although this book mentions a lot of graphic novels, it only scratches the surface. One of the most valuable things about interdisciplinary teaching is the opportunity to share resources. When an interdisciplinary unit is still in the planning stages, teachers should put the word out among disciplinary colleagues that they are looking for graphic novel resources. Don't be afraid to ask students to help in the search as well.

Remember that interdisciplinary units involve covering new ground. Students may find resources that don't prove to be useful. They may also discover resources that may take your interdisciplinary research in a different direction than expected. If this happens, it does not equal failure. On the contrary, discovering that which one did not expect is the whole point of interdisciplinary study. When looking at the spaces between categories, one often has the opportunity to discover what no one else has seen, but one has to be open to seeing it.

CRITICAL RESPONSE

In interdisciplinary teaching, it is a wonderful thing for students to be able to share what they have discovered with others, and having students make a graphic novel can be one option for a culminating activity. As we mentioned in previous chapters, many teachers assume that if a unit includes graphic novels, then the culminating activity must require students to make their own graphic novel. Consider, though, do teachers require students who have just finished a unit involving textbooks to write a textbook?

While there is a great deal that can be learned by having students create a graphic novel, and while a graphic novel might be a good way to engage your audience about important topics or issues, to do such an activity well requires a huge amount of time teaching students how graphic novels do what they do and requires students to have well-developed artistic and writing abilities. There is certainly value in offering the option to create a graphic novel as a way of sharing what students have learned—but be careful not to require this without considering the overall goals for the interdisciplinary unit.

Instead of concentrating on having students learn the skills necessary to create their own graphic novel, help students focus on the information and knowledge they have gained and the way in which they gained it. It is easy to overlook the knowledge gained from the visuals in graphic novels and from the interactions of the visuals and the text. Information gained from visuals is sometimes best presented in a visual format, which could include writing a graphic novel, but other options include producing a digital video, a music/ slideshow presentation, a web page, a live poster presentation night open to the public, and many other options.

Units that result in students generating new understandings (including project-based learning, integrated units, and interdisciplinary units, among other constructivist approaches) lend themselves to a culminating activity that involves disseminating what students learned. Besides the visual approaches mentioned before, podcasts, petitions, community awareness meetings, and writing letters to government officials are good ways for students to engage their community for change. It may be helpful to consider what sort of information or understanding the students uncover and what audience needs to hear about this information.

Some projects may uncover interesting information (e.g., an interdisciplinary unit between a biology class and a history class looking at survival challenges of Arctic and Antarctic exploration); some uncover information that could be important to a particular group (e.g., an interdisciplinary unit involving a business class and a Spanish class that work together to offer basic tax help to non-English speakers); and some dig into information that carries with it a social justice imperative to take action on an even bigger scale (e.g., an integrated unit that looks at human trafficking in a large metropolitan area).

A discussion with students about the type of information they wish to disseminate and the audience they have in mind will help narrow the list of possible culminating activities. In the case of the first example about survival in the cold, since the information is certainly interesting but not vital to be targeted to a particular group, presentations to parents, community, or fellow students would be fine. That information (involving scientific data and pictures as well as text) might lend itself to a multimodal format (website, poster, presentation software, or even a graphic novel if students have the skill, interest, and time).

In the case of the second suggestion, while a demonstration video or graphic novel is a possibility, because the target audience has different tax situations and different levels of familiarity with English, it might be most effective to hold a clinic and offer one-on-one help.

In the third example, one high school tackling this problem decided that what was most important was to change people's attitudes toward prostitution in their city. Students designed an art exhibit for a local gallery. Students added bruises and scars to Barbie dolls and then repackaged them in boxes that included information about local statistics, descriptions of the lives of people who were victims of human trafficking, and even suggestions on how the viewer could help.

So using graphic novels in the research of a topic is an excellent way to help students to engage with and learn about a topic. Graphic novels also can be a good option for a culminating activity, but never force students to attempt such a challenging task if there are other, more effective ways to convey what they have learned to an audience.

CONCLUSION: WHAT DID WE LEARN?

Using graphic novels in interdisciplinary teaching can bridge interest and engagement from one discipline to another, can allow students to practice transferring skills and understandings from one discipline to another, and can allow students to practice using distributed knowledge in problem solving. Graphic novels can be effective both as anchor texts and supporting texts. Graphic novels can support disciplinary ways of thinking with text, images, and the intersection of the two. Graphic novels can also cover the overlap between disciplines.

For effective interdisciplinary teaching, teachers should model reading graphic novels, give students the chance to identify affordances and constraints of graphic novels, and, finally, give students the opportunity to select, read, and evaluate graphic novels to find useful knowledge.

Critical response activities should provide opportunities for students to share the knowledge they have learned in a multimodal way, but should not be limited to requiring all students to share their learnings in the form of a graphic novel. Instead, teachers and students should work together to determine the most effective way to share what they have learned.

Chapter Ten

Putting It All Together

*Using Graphic Novels to Support
Disciplinary Literacies Instruction*

Throughout the book, graphic novels have shown a multitude of affordances for supporting disciplinary literacies instruction. Ultimately, though, it is you, the teacher, who will need to decide how to choose instruction goals, which graphic novels to integrate with other text resources, which disciplinary approach to take, how to help students see picture/text hybridity, how to frame inquiry, and which graphic novels provide the best opportunities for critical response.

As you embark on using graphic novels in your classes, you can use graphic novels not simply as supplemental texts, but also systematically to deepen disciplinary learning. To be systematic, consider the following suggestions for moving forward:

1. Become an avid reader of graphic novels.
2. Share your experiences using graphic novels with colleagues.
3. Engage in action research about your use of graphic novels for disciplinary learning.

BECOME AN AVID READER OF GRAPHIC NOVELS

The first question teachers might ask is, "As new graphic novels come out, how can I learn which ones might be best for my classroom?" There are a few resources that can serve as guides to reading and determining the potential for classroom use. First, below is a list of resources with a list of the top

121

resources for use in each discipline. These are not simply a list of our favorites, but a collection of award-winning graphic novels that can strengthen disciplinary literacies instruction (see textbox 10.1).

Second, the Internet contains a number of sites that review graphic novels. We recommend following one or two of them: One of this book's authors (Bill) maintains a blog called *Book Commercials*. The site, http://bookcommercial.blogspot.com, contains reviews of hundreds of graphic novels (and other young adult literature) from the perspective of how suitable they are for classroom use. A second site is *Graphic Novel Resources*, http://graphicnovelresources.blogspot.com, authored by Dr. Stergios Botzakis from the University of Tennessee. Finally, the blog *No Flying No Tights*, http://noflyingnotights.com, also publishes reviews of current graphic novels. Popular media such as the *New York Times* often have special sections dedicated to the review of graphic novels.

Finally, there are academic journal outlets that review and research graphic novels. The *School Library Journal* regularly reviews graphic novels. The *Journal of Graphic Novels and Comics* and *SANE Journal: Sequential Art Narrative in Education* are peer-reviewed journals that focus on empirical and theoretical studies using graphic novels. As a critical consumer of graphic novels yourself, you can better position yourself and your students to use them for disciplinary learning. Graphic novels will continue to proliferate and be integral to instruction.

Textbox 10.1 Graphic Novel Recommendations

Top Five Graphic Novels for Teaching about Health Issues

Arnoldi, K. (1998). *The amazing true story of a teenage single mom.* New York, NY: Hyperion. Black-and-white drawings and a compelling and honest voice take us through the desperation and frightening aspects of being a young, single mother, but also share hopes, perseverance, and ultimately triumph.

Fies, B. (2006). *Mom's cancer.* New York, NY: Abrams. Drawn in a style that seems to ride the edge between realism and caricature, this book takes the reader on a journey through the roller coaster of cancer and how it affects the three grown children of the mom who is diagnosed.

Jamieson, V. (2015). *Roller girl.* New York, NY: Penguin. This graphic novel was probably written for middle school–aged kids, but may be a relaxing read for high school students as well. The main character, Astrid, watches a Roller Derby match and decides she wants to play, too. That journey doesn't go as smoothly as she thinks it will. This is a good story about the importance of persistence.

Marchetto, M. A. (2006). *Cancer vixen.* New York, NY: Knopf. When the title character gets cancer, she faces it with attitude and frankness, but over the course of the book, she moves from a somewhat shallow life to a more committed one. Vulgar language could cause this book to be challenged.

Winick, J. (2000). *Pedro and me: Friendship, loss, and what I learned.* New York, NY: Henry Holt. Judd develops a friendship with Pedro who has (and eventually dies of) AIDS/HIV, while they are living in a communal house as part of the reality show *MTV's Real World.*

Top Ten Graphic Novels for Teaching History

Getz, T. R., & Clarke, L. (2012). *Abina and the important men.* New York, NY: Oxford. This beautifully illustrated graphic novel tells the story of a young African woman in 1876 sold by her husband to be a servant in the household of a wealthy planter. With the help of an African court translator, she appealed to the court of law. This graphic novel also features sections including court transcripts, explanations of political and social context, and other useful resources to inform students' understandings of the event.

Johnson, M., & Pleece, W. (2008). *Incognegro.* New York, NY: Vertigo. This fictional but well-researched story concerns a black reporter who can pass for white and uses this to pose as a white photographer who takes pictures of people standing next to lynching victims. He then takes the pictures back to Harlem and writes about the event. After a close call, he decides to retire, but then his editor suggests he investigate one last planned lynching—that of his half brother.

Laird, R., & Bey, E. (1997). *Still I rise: A cartoon history of African Americans.* New York, NY: Norton. This graphic novel features two elderly African American narrators, a man and a woman, each of whom use the scope of history to make a point. The man argues that, overall, things have gotten better for African Americans. The woman argues the opposite. This well-researched book can serve as a good introduction to analyzing historical arguments.

Lewis, J., Aydin, A., & Powell, N. (2013–2016). *March: Books I, II,* and *III.* Excellent art, a fascinating narrative, and a first-person account of the civil rights movement from the ground floor combine to make Congressman John Lewis's memoir an excellent way to add life and personal connection to a gripping period of history.

Mizuki, S. (2013). *Showa 1926–1939: A history of Japan.* Montreal, QC: Drawn and Quarterly. This brilliant (but weighty at 553 pages) manga-style graphic novel tells the story of the economic and political struggles of prewar Japan and what led to the alliance with Germany in World War II. The book alternates between giving us the larger national picture, and seeing how those decisions affected everyday people—as seen through autobiographical chapters from Mizuki.

O'Connor, G. (2006). *Journey into Mohawk Country.* New York, NY: First Second. The words are the journal of a Dutch explorer, Harmen M. van den Bogaert, tasked with finding out why the Mohawk people were more apt to trade with the French than with the Dutch—something he seems to have utterly failed to determine. O'Connor's images, though, tell another story as van den Bogaert repeatedly engages in culturally insensitive acts. Though O'Connor's gloss on the journal is speculative, it may help students see how interpretive layers on first-person accounts work.

Sacco, J. (2002). *Safe area Gorazde.* Seattle, WA: Fantagraphics. At first, Joe Sacco's caricatured drawings might seem inappropriate for reportage about the Bosnian War, but as you read on, you discover they serve several purposes. Because he is drawing the subjects he is interviewing rather than photographing them, they are much more willing to talk candidly. His style also allows him to depict a range of emotions effectively, from desperation to the strange moments of humor that can accompany such situations. This graphic novel contains many first-person accounts.

Sturm, J., & Tommaso, R. (2007). *Satchel Paige: Striking out Jim Crow.* New York, NY: Hyperion. Though this book is written to be accessible to upper elementary and older, it is a fascinating tale of Satchel Paige and the Negro Leagues for any age. There is a fictional framing story; much of the material reads like a biography of Paige.

Vansant, W. (2013). *Bombing Nazi Germany: The graphic history of the Allied air campaign that defeated Hitler in World War Two.* Minneapolis, MN: Zenith. The images in this graphic novel will grab students' attention, and the drama of the Allied air campaign will hold them rapt, but along the way they will learn about Allied and German strategies, about the ways in which the air war was effective and ways it was not, and about the atrocities committed by both sides.

Zinn, H., Konopacki, M., & Buhle, P. (2008). *A people's history of American empire.* New York, NY: Metropolitan Books. Zinn looks at American history from the perspective of those who did not win battles, treaties, or agreements. The result is usually critical of American actions and apt to start interesting discussions. This adaptation of Zinn's original textbook is arguably less historically rigorous and more representative of opinion, but it will still result in good discussions.

Top Five Graphic Novels For Teaching Science

Hosler, J. (2000). *Clan Apis.* Columbus, OH: Active Synapse. This realistically illustrated graphic novel traces the life cycle of a honeybee, which does not sound as utterly fascinating and gripping as the actual story turns out to be. Hosler approaches the subject with a scientist's fascination.

Hosler, J. (2003). *The sandwalk adventures.* Columbus, OH: Active Synapse. Two mites that live in a hair follicle in Charles Darwin's beard have a discussion with him about evolutionary theory (seriously). While Hosler's other work is much more about the mechanics of natural selection, this book focuses on evolutionary theory and its implications for how to think about the biological world.

Hosler, J., Cannon, K., & Cannon, Z. (2011). *Evolution: The story of life on earth.* New York, NY: Hill and Wang. An alien scientist explains genetics and evolutionary theory to his somewhat hapless leader. Hosler's Ph.D. in biology and interest in storytelling combine for a wonderfully engaging and full explanation of life on earth.

Ottaviani, J. (1999). *Dignifying science: Stories about women scientists.* Ann Arbor, MI: GT Labs. This book is a series of biographies of women who have made a significant contribution to science, including Hedy Lamarr, Lise Meitner, Rosalind Franklin, Barbara McClintock, and Birute Galdikas. An excellent resource for encouraging female science students (and broadening the minds of some male students as well).

Ottaviani, J., & Purvis, L. (2004). *Suspended in language: Niels Bohr's life, discoveries, and the century he shaped.* Ann Arbor, MI: GT Labs. This graphic novel would be perfect for a high school physics class. The book describes theories and how they came to be in the context of Bohr's life.

Top Five Graphic Novels For Teaching Math

Andriopoulos, T., & Gkiokas, T. (2015). *Who killed Professor X?* New York, NY: Birkhauser. When a famous German mathematician dies during a Paris math conference, an inspector must get statements from all the mathematicians who are suspects—but often they explain their whereabouts during the crime in terms of geometry or other mathematical language. The reader can use their statements and the diagrams embedded in the story to try to figure out who the murderer is.

Colfer, E., Donkin, A., Rigano, G., & Lamanna, P. (2009). *Artemis Fowl: The Arctic incident.* London: Penguin. While some math teachers are drawn to the Artemis Fowl series because of its use of cryptography, there is also a fair amount of logic in each story—which mathematicians can point out to students.

Doxiadis, A., Papadimitriou, C. H., Papadatos, A., & Di Donna, A. (2009). *Logicomix: An epic search for truth.* New York, NY: Bloomsbury. This excellent story about the life of Bertrand Russell and his attempt to discover truth through mathematics, philosophy, and physics displays the creative team's skill, especially in working with panel-to-panel transitions. It contains some wonderful descriptions and explanations of geometry, paradox, and infinity; it also has a fair amount of secrets, scandals, madness, and mystery.

Ottaviani, J., Cannon, Z., & Cannon, K. (2009). *T-Minus: The race to the moon.* New York, NY: Aladdin. Astronauts are often seen as the heroes of the space race. This graphic novel shows the true heroes—the engineers and mathematicians that made it happen. The art in this book masterfully renders the story in a way that is spellbinding and gripping.

Yang, G. L., Holmes, M. (2015). *Secret coders.* New York, NY: First Second. This is actually a series of graphic novels about a girl named Hopper and her friend Eni whose skills at coding lead them to outwit a possibly evil janitor, control a robot, and have other adventures. The first book in the series includes the most useful explanation of binary coding that I have ever read—and does so squarely within the context of the story.

Top Eight Graphic Novel Adaptations of Classic Literature for Teaching English Language Arts

Bingham, J. (1984). *Beowulf.* Chicago, IL: First. Beowulf has always been kind of an action-adventure comic book story. Bingham embraces that idea. His hypermuscular heroes, grotesque monsters, and bikini-clad women seem to fit with the epic poem's story line. These is a lot here to interrogate.

Conan Doyle, A., Culbard, I. N. J., & Edginton, I. (2010). *Study in scarlet: A Sherlock Holmes graphic novel.* New York, NY: Sterling. The visuals in this adaptation (which tend a bit toward cartoonish caricature) provide a useful additional set of context clues to help with Conan Doyle's sometimes difficult prose. Given the recent interest in Sherlock Holmes due to the movie and television adaptations, this one might be a good choice.

Hinds, G. (2007). *William Shakespeare's King Lear.* The Comic.com. Nothing flashy here, but Hinds as always shows incredible skill at capturing the heart of whatever classic he is adapting. This is the next best thing to taking your students to see a live production.

Hinds, G. (2010). *The odyssey.* Somerville, MA: Candlewick. Hinds gets it. This is the Odyssey. He captures the blinding of the Cyclops, the sirens, the Book of the Dead, and best of all, Odysseus getting his revenge on the freeloading suitors.

Kafka, F, & Kuper, P. (2001). *The metamorphosis.* New York, NY: Three Rivers. Kuper's art is sort of gothic, involves a lot of shadows, and is perfect for Kafka's classic short story about Gregor Samsa who awakens one morning to find he has been turned into a giant bug.

Larsen, H. (2012). *Madeleine L'Engle's A wrinkle in time: The graphic novel.* New York, NY: Farrar, Straus and Giroux. It may be debatable whether this book counts as a classic, but I am including it here because I often think that Larsen's adaptation is better than the Newbery-winning original (which is sometimes underdescribed and hard to picture) and still manages to capture everything that is wonderful about that book.

Manga Shakespeare Series, New York, NY: Amulet. This series is interesting. They do a nice job of dramatizing the plays, and often show them in modern or fanciful settings (*King Lear* among Native American tribes, *Macbeth* in postapocalyptic Tokyo, etc.). This series won't connect with every student, but many of them will find the series compelling.

O'Connor, G. *The Olympians* series. New York, NY: First Second. Excellent artwork and panel design combine with O'Connor's well-researched stories to present the stories of the Greek gods. Supplemental material at the back of the book points out intertextual references and how O'Connor made decisions about portrayals and story lines. An excellent companion to any study of the *Iliad*, *Odyssey*, or *Aeneid*.

Top Five Contemporary Literary Graphic Novels for Teaching English Language Arts

Hicks, F. E. (2012). *Friends with boys.* New York, NY: First Second. Maggie has been homeschooled her whole life and now is starting high school. She worries about finding friends and finding her classes. Fortunately, her oldest brother and twin middle brothers are there to help. Now if only she weren't haunted by a ghost. Themes include developing identity, defining friendship, and developing courage by standing up to what you fear.

Phelan, M. (2013). *Bluffton: My summers with Buster.* Somerville, MA: Candlewick. Henry thinks there isn't much remarkable about Muskegon, Michigan, where he is growing up, until a group of vaudeville performers begin summering at the cottages up the road. Henry meets Buster, a young performer who can juggle and do some magic, but is best at pratfalls. When both of them take a liking to Henry's neighbor Sally, things get interesting. This is a heartwarming story with a twist at the end. Might be useful in connection with a cinema class.

Talbot, B. (1995). *The tale of one bad rat.* Milwaukie, OR: Dark Horse. This is an amazing story about a young girl on the run from a sexually abusive household and how she finds friendship and healing. Many intertextual references to the Beatrix Potter books.

Vaughan, B. K., & Henrichon, N. (2006). *Pride of Baghdad.* New York, NY: DC. During the bombing of Iraq by American forces, four lions escape from the Baghdad Zoo. Told from the lions' point of view, this graphic novel has a lot to say about the randomness and senselessness of war. Good for pairing with *All Quiet on the Western Front* or *The Things They Carried.*

Yang, G. (2006). *American born Chinese.* New York, NY: First Second. A sophisticated exploration of a young Chinese American boy trying to figure out his identity in terms of the cultures he stands between. Excellent.

SHARE YOUR EXPERIENCES

As you embark on using graphic novels for disciplinary learning, it is helpful to your colleagues if you share your experiences. Discussing how you are using graphic novels helps to demystify their role. Share these experiences and student work with grade-level team members and your departments. Other ways you can share are by blogging about your classroom projects or tweeting to your professional learning network. Since graphic novel use in the disciplines is a fairly recent phenomenon, examples and shared experiences are needed.

Sharing with others not only supports colleagues but provides extended opportunities to reflect and be metacognitive of your own instructional practices. Deciding what to share, how to share, and when to share all require extended reflection on what happened in the classroom. Deep and critical reflections on your practice can lead to improvements for future lessons.

ENGAGE IN ACTION RESEARCH

To teach well with graphic novels, it is also important to reflect on your teaching. Action research projects are a great way to investigate the use of graphic novels for disciplinary learning. As you may know, action research includes a focus on a problem or issue, a systematic process of inquiry, and development of explanations that leads to increased understanding you can then act upon (Stringer et al., 2014). Action research lets you investigate questions about how using graphic novels to teach for disciplinary literacy is impacting students. Most importantly, the findings from action research studies provide evidence for sound instructional improvements.

Possible research questions may include:

- How do students' scientific explanations of evolutionary theory change after reading *The Sandwalk Adventures*?
- What features of graphic novels are most motivating to students in their disciplinary study?
- What elements of *March I & II* do students corroborate with primary source material in their historical interpretation of the civil rights movement?
- How well do students recognize literary devices such as characterization and narrator reliability when reading *American Born Chinese*?

There are several questions you can investigate through your use of action research. The purpose, however, is to use the information gained to inform future theories of action when using graphic novels in your classroom. Results from action research studies can be powerful when convincing those who are skeptical of their use or effectiveness in the classroom.

LOOKING FORWARD

However you decide to integrate graphic novels into your disciplinary instruction, remember that the GRAPHIC framework is a tool for planning and not a formula or step-by-step guide to using graphic novels. The framework can help support and guide your disciplinary instruction and help you harness graphic novels as powerful texts. As such, graphic novels are not simply additive. Nor should they be used like a condiment to "spice up" traditional teaching (Kim, 2011) without deep considerations in changing pedagogy or frameworks.

Graphic novels, like all great literature, multiply our perspectives and provide windows, mirrors, and sliding glass doors into the disciplines (Sims Bishop, 1990). That is, graphic novels open unique opportunities for youth to garner multiple perspectives, alternative explanations, counternarratives, and pathways to disciplinary learning that are limited with traditional-printed text.

Disciplinary literacies instruction can empower youth to critically engage with their world. The use of texts such as graphic novels to develop those habits of thinking, the cultural tools, habits of practice, and ways of knowing are critical. Our young people deserve opportunities to read and write the word and the world as critical agents and as critical citizens. Graphic novels are an essential resource for doing so.

Works Cited

Arlin, M., & Roth, G. (1978). Pupils' use of time while reading comics and books. *American Educational Research Journal, 15*(2), 201–216.

Arnett, D. (2008). Implementing graphic texts into the language arts classroom. *Minnesota English Journal, 44*(1), 150–179.

Baker, A. (2011). *Using comics to improve literacy in English language learners* (Master's thesis). University of Central Mississippi.

Bazerman, C. (1985). Physicists reading physics schema-laden purposes and purpose-laden schema. *Written Communication, 2*(1), 3–23.

Boatright, M. D. (2010). Graphic journeys: Graphic novels' representations of immigrant experiences. *Journal of Adolescent & Adult Literacy, 53*(6), 468–476.

Boerman-Cornell, W. (2010). History is relatives: Educational affordances of the graphic novel in *The magical life of Long Tack Sam. International Journal of Comic Arts, 12*(1), 147–156.

Boerman-Cornell, W. (2011). Graphic novels for the classroom: Affordances for using graphic novels to teach high school history. In B. Carrington and J. Harding (Eds.), *Going graphic: Comics and graphic novels for young people.* Lichfield, UK: Pied Piper.

Boerman-Cornell, W. (2013). Exploring the text/image wilderness: Ironic visual perspective and critical thinking in George O'Connor's graphic novel *Journey into Mohawk Country. Bookbird, 51*(4), 29–34.

Boerman-Cornell, W. (2015). Using historical graphic novels in high school history classes: Potential for contextualization, sourcing, and corroborating. *History Teacher, 48*(2), 209–224.

Botzakis, S. (2011). To be part of the dialogue: American adults reading comic books. *Journal of Graphic Novels and Comic Books*, 113–123.

Bridges, E. (2009). Bridging the gap: A literacy-oriented approach to teaching the novel *Der Este Fruhlung. Der Unterrichtspraxis / Teaching German, 42*(2), 152–161.

Brozo, W. G., Moorman, G., & Meyer, C. K. (2013). *Wham! Teaching with graphic novels across the curriculum.* New York: Teachers College Press.

Callahan, R. (2009). *Perceptions and use of graphic novels in the classroom* (Master's thesis). Ohio University.

Carter, J. B. (2007). Are there any Hester Prynnes in our world today? Pairing *The amazing true story of a teenage single mom* with *The scarlet letter.* In James Bucky Carter (Ed.), *Building literacy connections with graphic novels: Page by page, panel by panel.* Urbana, IL: NCTE.

Cavazos-Kottke, S. (2006). Five readers browsing: The reading interests of talented middle school boys. *Gifted Child Quarterly, 30*(2), 132–147.

Chang, J. C. (2011). *Reading between the frames: English language learners and non-English language learners' responses to graphic novels* (Master's thesis). University of Toronto.

Chun, C. (2009). Critical literacies and graphic novels for English language learners: Teaching *Maus*. *Journal of Adolescent & Adult Literacy, 53*(2),144–153.

Clark, J. S. (2013). Encounters with historical agency: The value of nonfiction graphic novels in the classroom. *History Teacher, 46*(4), 489–508.

Connors, S. P. (2012). Altering perspectives: How the implied reader invites us to rethink the difficulty of graphic novels. *Clearing House, 85*, 33–37.

Cooper, S., Nesmith, S., & Schwartz, G. (2011). Exploring graphic novels for elementary science and mathematics. *School Library Research, 14*, 1–16.

Cope, B., & Kalantzis, M. (2009). "Multiliteracies": New literacies, new learning. *Pedagogies: An International Journal, 4*(3), 164–195.

Crawford, P. (2009). A novel approach: Using graphic novels to attract reluctant readers. *Literary Media Connection, 34*(1), 36–38.

Cromer, M., & Clark, P. (2007). Getting graphic with the past: Graphic novels and the teaching of history. *Theory and Research in Social Education, 35*(4), 574–591.

Csikszentmihalyi, M. (1997). *Finding flow: The psychology of engagement with everyday life.* New York: Basic Books.

Decker, A. C., & Castro, M. (2012). Teaching history with comic books: A case study of violence, war, and the graphic novel. *History Teacher, 45*(2), 170–187.

Doran, C. M. (2008). Reading right to left: How defamiliarizaton helps students read a familiar genre. In Colin C. Irvine (Ed.), *Teaching the novel across the curriculum: A handbook for educators* (pp. 118–129). Westport, CT: Greenwood.

Droste, S. (2012). *Self-improvement hypothesis in graphic novels* (Doctoral dissertation). Retrieved from ProQuest.

Dulaney, M. (2012). *Graphic narratives: Cognitive and pedagogical choices from implementation in the English language arts classroom* (Doctoral dissertation). North Carolina State University.

Fisher, D., & Frey, N. (2007). Altering English: Re-examining the whole class novel and making room for graphic novels and more. In James Bucky Carter (Ed.), *Building literacy connections with graphic novels: Page by page, panel by panel.* Urbana, IL: NCTE.

Frey, N., & Fisher, D. (2004). Using graphic novels, anime, and the Internet in an urban high school. *English Journal, 93*(3), 19–25.

Gavigan, K. W. (2011). More powerful than a locomotive: Using graphic novels to motivate struggling male adolescent readers. *Journal of Research on Literature and Young Adults, 1*(3).

Gee, J. P. (2014). *What video games have to teach us about learning and literacy.* New York: Macmillan.

Gillenwater, C. (2012). *Graphic novels in advanced English/language arts classrooms: A phenomenological study* (Doctoral dissertation). Retrieved from ProQuest.

Goldman, S. R., Britt, M. A., Brown, W., Cribb, G., George, M., Greenleaf, C., Lee, C. D., Shanahan, C., & Project READ. (2016). Disciplinary literacies and learning to read for understanding: A conceptual framework for disciplinary literacy. *Educational Psychology, 51*(2), 219–246.

Gomes, C., & Carter, J. B. (2010). Navigating through social norms, negotiating place: How *American born Chinese* motivates struggling readers. *English Journal, 100*(2), 68–76.

Gray, W. S. (1925). Reading activities in school and in social life. In G. M. Whipple (Ed.), *The twenty-fourth yearbook of the National Society for the Study of Education, part I* (pp. 1–8). Bloomington, IL: Public School Publishing.

Green, M. J. (2013). Teaching with comics: A course for fourth year medical students. *Journal of Medical Humanities, 34*(4), 471–476.

Griffith, P. E. (2010). Graphic novels in the secondary classroom and school libraries. *Journal of Adolescent & Adult Literacy, 54*(3), 181–189.

Guzzetti, B. (2009). Thinking like a forensic scientist: Learning with academic and everyday texts. *Journal of Adolescent & Adult Literacy, 53*(3), 192–203.

Hammond, H. (2012). Graphic novels and multimodal literacy: A high school study with *American born Chinese. Bookbird, 50*(4), 22–32.

Hammond, H. K. (2009). *Graphic novels and multimodal literacy: A reader-response study* (Doctoral dissertation). University of Minnesota.

Heisler, F. (1948). A comparison between those elementary school children who attend moving pictures, read comic books and listen to serial radio programs to an excess, with those who indulge in these activities seldom or not at all. *Journal of Educational Research, 42*(3), 182–190.

Herber, H. L. (1970). *Teaching reading in the content areas.* Englewood Cliffs, NJ: Prentice Hall.

Hughes, J. M., King, A., Perkins, P., & Fuke, V. (2011). Adolescents and "autographics": Reading and writing coming-of-age graphic novels. *Journal of Adolescent & Adult Literacy, 54*(8), 601–612.

Hughes-Hassell, S., & Rodge, P. (2007). The leisure reading habits of urban adolescents. *Journal of Adolescent & Adult Literacy, 51*(1), 22–33.

Jimenez, L. M., & Meyer, C. K. (2016). First impressions matter: Navigating graphic novels utilizing linguistic, visual, and spatial resources. *Journal of Literacy Research, 48*(4), 423–447.

Juneau, T., & Sucharov, M. (2010). Narratives in pencil: Using graphic novels to teach Israeli-Palestinian relations. *International Studies Perspectives, 11*, 172–183.

Kim, J. (2011). Is it bigger than hip-hop?: Examining the problems and potential of hip-hop in the curriculum. In V. Kinloch (Ed.), *Urban literacies: Critical perspectives on education in urban settings* (160–176). New York: Teachers College Press.

Krashen, S. D. (2004). *The power of reading: Insights from the research* (2nd ed.). Westport, CT: Libraries Unlimited.

Lamanno, A. A. (2007). *Exploring the use of graphic novels in the classroom: Does exposure to non-traditional texts increase the reading comprehension skills and motivation of low-functioning adolescent readers?* (Doctoral dissertation). Pennsylvania State University.

Lapp, D., Wolsey, T. D., Fisher, D., & Frey, N. (2011–2012). Graphic novels: What elementary teachers think about their educational value. *Journal of Education, 192*(1), 23–35.

Leckbee, J. (2005). I got graphic: Using visual literacy works. *Young Adult Library,* 30–31.

Lee, C. D. (2014). The multi-dimensional demands of reading in the disciplines. *Journal of Adolescent & Adult Literacy, 58*(1), 9–15.

Manderino, M., & Wickens, C. M. (2014). Addressing disciplinary literacy in the Common Core State Standards. *Illinois Reading Council Journal, 42*(2), 28–39.

Martinez-Roldan, C. M., & Newcomer, S. (2011). Reading between the pictures: Immigrant students' impressions of *The arrival. Language Arts, 88*(3), 188–197.

McCloud, S. (1994). *Understanding comics: The invisible art.* New York: William Morrow.

McConachie, S. M., & Petrosky, A. R. (2010). *Content matters: A disciplinary literacy approach to improving student learning.* San Francisco, CA: Wiley.

Moeller, R. (2008). *"No thanks, these are boy books": A feminist cultural analysis of graphic novels as curricular materials* (Doctoral dissertation). Retrieved from ProQuest.

Monnin, K. (2008). *Perceptions of new literacies with the graphic novel* Bone (Doctoral dissertation). Retrieved from ProQuest.

Monnin, K. (2009). Breaking into the superhero boy's club: Teaching graphic novel literary heroines in secondary English language arts. *Women in Literacy and Life Assembly of the National Council of Teachers of English Assembly Journal, 17*, 20–25.

O'Brien, D. G., Stewart, R. A., & Moje, E. B. (1995). Why content literacy is difficult to infuse into the secondary school: Complexities of curriculum, pedagogy, and school culture. *Reading Research Quarterly, 30*(3), 442–463.

Pantaleo, S. (2011). Warning: A grade 7 student disrupts narrative boundaries. *Journal of Literacy Research, 43*(1), 39–67.

Schieble, M. (2011). A case for interruption in the virtual English classroom with the graphic novel *American born Chinese. Australian Journal of Language and Literacy, 34*(2), 202–218.

Schraffenberger, J. D. (2007). Visualizing Beowulf: Old English gets graphic. In James Bucky Carter (Ed.), *Building literacy connections with graphic novels: Page by page, panel by panel.* Urbana, IL: NCTE.

Schoenbach, R., Greenleaf, C., & Murphy, L. (2012). *Reading for understanding: How reading apprenticeship improves disciplinary learning in secondary and college classrooms.* Hoboken, NJ: John Wiley and Sons.

Schwartz, G. (2006). Expanding literacies through graphic novels. *English Journal, 95*(6), 58–64.

Seelow, D. (2010). The graphic novel as advanced literary tool. *Journal of Media Literacy Education, 2*(1), 57–64.

Shipwright, S., Mallory, D., Atack, L., & Demacio, P. (2010). An online graphic novel: Students' experiences and research literacy gains. *MERLOT: Journal of Online Teaching and Learning, 6*(3), 573–584.

Sims Bishop, R. (1990). Mirrors, windows, and sliding glass doors. *Perspectives, 1*(3), ix–xi.

Smetana, L., Odelson, D., Burns, H., & Grisham, D. (2009). Using graphic novels in the high school classroom: Engaging deaf students with a new genre. *Journal of Adolescent & Adult Literacy, 53*(3), 228–240.

Snowball, C. (2008). Teenagers talking about reading and libraries. *Australian Academic and Research Libraries, 39*(2), 106–118.

Stringer, E. T., Agrello, M. F., Baldwin, S. C., Christensen, L. M., & Henry, D. L. P. (2014). *Community based ethnography: Breaking traditional boundaries of research, teaching, and learning.* Hove, UK: Psychology Press.

Swain, E. H. (1978). Using comic books to teach reading and language arts. *Journal of Reading, 22*(3), 253–258.

Tatalovic, M. (2009). Science comics as tools for science education and communication: A brief expository study. *Journal of Science Education, 8*(4), AO2.

Warrican, S. J. (2006). Promoting reading amidst repeated failure: Meeting the challenges. *High School Journal, 90*(1), 33–43.

Wertham, F. (1954). *Seduction of the innocent: The influence of comic books on today's youth.* New York: Rinehart.

White, B. (2011). The world in words and pictures: How graphic novels can help to increase reading comprehension for students with hearing loss. *Knowledge Quest, 39*(3), 18–25.

Wickens, C. M., Manderino, M., Parker, J., & Jung, J. (2015). Habits of practice. *Journal of Adolescent & Adult Literacy, 59*(1), 75–82.

Williams, I. C. W. (2012). Graphic medicine: Comics as medical narrative. *Medical Humanities, 38*(1), 21–27.

Wineburg, S. S. (1991). Historical problem solving: A study of the cognitive processes used in the evaluation of documentary and pictorial evidence. *Journal of Educational Psychology, 83*(1), 73–87.

Witty, P. (1941). Children's interest in reading the comics. *Journal of Experimental Education, 10*(2), 100–104.

Witty, P., & Sizemore, R. A. (1955). Reading the comics: A summary of studies and an evaluation. *Elementary English, 32*, 109–114.

GRAPHIC NOVELS REFERENCED

Anderson, H. C. (1993). *King 1 and 2.* Seattle, WA: Fantagraphics.

Andriopoulos, T., & Gkiokas, T. (2015). *Who killed Professor X?* New York: Birkhauser.

Arnoldi, K. (1998). *The amazing true story of a teenage single mom.* New York: Hyperion.

Ayers, W., & Alexander-Tanner, R. (2010). *To teach: The journey, in comics.* New York: Teachers College Press.

B., D. (2006). *Epileptic.* New York: Pantheon.

Baker, K. (2006). *Nat Turner.* New York: Abrams.

Bechdel, A. (2007). *Fun home: A tragicomic.* New York: Mariner Books.

Bell, C. (2014). *El deafo.* New York: Abrams.

Bellstorf, A. (2012). *Baby's in Black: Astrid Kirchherr, Stuart Sutcliffe, and the Beatles.* New York: First Second.

Bingham, J. (1984). *Beowulf.* Chicago, IL: First.

Buhle, P., Pekar, H., & Piskor, E. (2009). *The Beats: A graphic history.* London: Souvenir.

Castellucci, C. (2007). *The Plain Janes.* New York: Minx.

Colfer, E., Donkin, A., Rigano, G., & Lamanna, P. (2009). *Artemis Fowl: The Arctic incident.* London: Penguin.

Conan Doyle, A., Culbard, I. N. J., & Edginton, I. (2010). *A Study in scarlet: A Sherlock Holmes graphic novel.* New York: Sterling.

Deas, R., & Shakespeare, W. (2008). *Manga Shakespeare: Macbeth.* New York: Amulet.

Disco, J., Clark, S., & Singleton, N. (2011). *Echoes of the Lost Boys of Sudan.* Dallas, TX: Brown Books.

Doxiadis, A., Papadimitriou, C. H., Papadatos, A., & Di Donna, A. (2009). *Logicomix: An epic search for truth.* London: Bloomsbury.

El Rassi, T. (2007). *Arab in America.* San Francisco, CA: Last Gasp.

Fies, B. (2006). *Mom's cancer.* New York: Abrams.

Gaiman, N. (2010). *Sandman: Preludes and nocturnes.* New York: Vertigo.

Getz, T. R., & Clarke, L. (2012). *Abina and the important men.* New York: Oxford.

Gill, J. C. (2014). *Strange fruit: Uncelebrated narratives from black history.* Golden, CO: Fulcrum.

Gladstone, B. (2011). *The influencing machine.* New York: Norton.

Gunderson, J., & Hayden, S. (2011). X: A biography of Malcolm X. Chicago, IL: Capstone.

Halliday, A., & Hoppe, P. (2013). *Peanut.* New York: Schwartz and Wade.

Hatke, B. (2016). *Mighty Jack.* New York: First Second.

Helfer, A. (2006). *Malcolm X: A graphic biography.* New York: Hill and Wang.

Hicks, F. E. (2012). *Friends with boys.* New York: First Second.

Hinds, G. (2007a). *Beowulf.* Somerville, MA: Candlewick.

Hinds, G. (2007b). *William Shakespeare's King Lear.* The Comic.Com.

Hinds, G. (2010). *The odyssey.* Somerville, MA: Candlewick.

Hornschemeier, P. (2009). *Mother, come home.* Seattle, WA: Fantagraphics.

Hosler, J. (2000). *Clan Apis.* Columbus, OH: Active Synapse.

Hosler, J. (2003). *The sandwalk adventures: An adventure in evolution told in five chapters.* Columbus, OH: Active Synapse.

Hosler, J. (2005). *The last of the sandwalkers.* New York: First Second.

Hosler, J. (2013). *Optical allusions.* CreateSpace Independent Publishing Platform.

Hosler, J., Cannon, K., & Cannon, Z. (2011). *Evolution: The story of life on earth.* New York: Hill and Wang.

Jamieson, V. (2015). *Roller girl.* New York: Penguin.

Johnson, M., & Pleece, W. (2008). *Incognegro.* New York: Vertigo.

Kafka, F., & Kuper, P. (2001). *The metamorphosis.* New York: Three Rivers.

Keller, M., & Rager Fuller, N. (2009). *Charles Darwin's On the origin of species.* New York: Rodale Books.

Kubert, J. (1996). *Fax from Sarajevo.* Milwaukie, OR: Dark Horse.

Laird, R., & Bey, E. (1997). *Still I rise: A cartoon history of African Americans.* New York: Norton.

Larson, H. (2012). *Madeleine L'Engle's A wrinkle in time: The graphic novel.* New York: Farrar, Straus and Giroux.

Lendler, I., & Giallongo, Z. (2014). *The Stratford Zoo Midnight Revue presents Macbeth.* New York: First Second.

Lewis, J., Aydin, A., & Powell, N. (2013). *March I.* Marietta, GA: Top Shelf.

Lewis, J., Aydin, A., & Powell, N. (2015). *March II.* Marietta, GA: Top Shelf.

Lewis, J., Aydin, A., & Powell, N. (2010). *March III.* Marietta, GA: Top Shelf.

Long, M., Demonakos, M., & Powell, N. (2012). *The silence of our friends: The civil rights struggle was never black and white.* New York: First Second.

Manga Shakespeare series. New York: Amulet.

Marchetto, M. A. (2006). *Cancer vixen.* New York: Knopf.

McCreery, C., & Del Col, A. (2010). *Kill Shakespeare: A sea of troubles.* San Diego, CA: IDW.

Mizuki, S. (2013). *Showa 1926–1939: A history of Japan.* Montreal, QC: Drawn and Quarterly.

Modan, R. (2008). *Exit wounds* (N. Stollman, Trans.). Montreal, QC: Drawn and Quarterly.

Moore, A. (1986). *Watchmen.* New York: DC.

Morales, R., & Baker, K. (2003). *Truth: Red, white, & black.* New York: Marvel.

Morvan, J.-D., Trefouel, S., & Bertail, D. (2015). *Omaha Beach on D-day.* New York: First Second.

Murphy, J., Milgrom, A., & Brown, J. (2008). *Cleburne: A graphic novel.* Jacksonville, FL: Rampart.

O'Connor, G. (2006). *Journey into Mohawk Country.* New York: First Second.

O'Connor, G. (2010–). *The Olympians* series. New York: First Second.

O'Connor, G. (2010). *Zeus: King of the gods.* New York: First Second.

Ottaviani, J. (1999). *Dignifying science: Stories about women scientists.* Ann Arbor, MI: G.T. Labs.

Ottaviani, J., Cannon, Z., & Cannon, K. (2009). *T-Minus: The race to the moon.* New York: Aladdin.

Ottaviani, J., & Myrick, L. (2011). *Feynman.* New York: First Second.

Ottaviani, J., & Purvis, L. (2009). *Suspended in language: Niels Bohr's life, discoveries, and the century he shaped.* Ann Arbor, MI: GT Labs.

Ottaviani, J., Schulz, M., Cannon, K., & Cannon, Z. (2004). *Bone sharps, cowboys, and thunder lizards.* Ann Arbor, MI: GT Labs.

Ottaviani, J., & Wicks, M. (2013). *Primates: The fearless science of Jane Goodall, Dian Fossey, and Biruté Galdikas.* New York: Macmillan.

Pekar, H., & Waldman, J. (2014). *Not the Israel my parents promised me.* New York: Hill and Wang.

Phelan, M. (2013). *Bluffton: My summer with Buster.* Somerville, MA: Candlewick.

Powell, N. (2008). *Swallow me whole.* Marietta, GA: Top Shelf.

Sacco, J. (2001). *Palestine.* Seattle, WA: Fantagraphics.

Sacco, J. (2002). *Safe area Gorazde.* Seattle, WA: Fantagraphics.

Sacco, J. (2009). *Footnotes in Gaza.* London: Jonathan Cope.

Santiago, W. (2011). *21: The story of Roberto Clemente.* Seattle, WA: Fantagraphics.

Satrapi, M. (2003). *Persepolis: The story of a childhood.* New York: Pantheon.

Schultz, M., Cannon, Z., & Cannon, K. (2009). *The stuff of life: A graphic guide to genetics and DNA.* New York: Hill and Wang.

Selznick, B. (2007). *The invention of Hugo Cabret.* New York: Scholastic.

Smith, J. (2005). *Bone #1: Out from Boneville.* New York: Scholastic.

Sousanis, N. (2015). *Unflattening.* Cambridge, MA: Harvard University Press.

Sperling, J. (2006). *Unknown soldier.* New York: DC.

Spiegelman, A. (1986). *Maus: A survivor's tale (I and II).* New York: Pantheon.

Stassen, J. P. (2006). *Deogratias.* New York: First Second.

Stevenson, N. (2015). *Nimona.* New York: HarperTeen.

Stevenson, N., Watters, S., & Allen, B. A. (2015). *Lumberjanes Volume 1: Beware the kitten holy.* Los Angeles, CA: BOOM! Box.

Sturm, J., & Tommaso, R. (2007). *Satchel Paige: Striking out Jim Crow.* New York: Hyperion.

Talbot, B. (1995). *The tale of one bad rat.* Milwaukie, OR: Dark Horse.

Tamaki, J., & Tamaki, M. (2014). *This One Summer.* New York: First Second.

Tan, S. (2006). *The arrival.* London: Hodder.

Thomas, R., & Sepulveda, M. A. (2008). *The iliad.* New York: Marvel.

VanSant, W. (2013). *Bombing Nazi Germany: The graphic history of the allied air campaign that defeated Hitler in World War II.* Minneapolis, MN: Zenith.

Vaughan, B. K., & Henrichon, N. (2006). *Pride of Baghdad.* New York: DC.

Wilson, G. W., & Alphona, A. (2015). *Ms. Marvel: No normal.* New York: Marvel.

Winick, J. (2000). *Pedro and me: Friendship, loss, and what I learned.* New York: Henry Holt.

Yang, G. (2006). *American born Chinese.* New York: First Second.

Yang, G. (2013). *Boxers.* New York: First Second.

Yang, G. (2013). *Saints*. New York: First Second.

Yang, G., & Holmes, M. (2015). *Secret coders*. New York: First Second.

Yang, G., & Holmes, M. (2016). *Secret coders: Paths and portals*. New York: First Second.

Yang, G., & Holmes, M. (2017). *Secret coders: Robots and repeats*. New York: First Second.

Yang, G., & Holmes, M. (2017). *Secret coders: Secrets and sequences*. New York: First Second.

Zimmerman, D. J., & Vansant, W. (2009). *The Vietnam War: A graphic history.* New York: Hill and Wang.

Zinn, H., Konopacki, D., & Buhle, P. (2008). *A people's history of American empire*. New York: Metropolitan Books, 2008.

25588948R00093

Made in the USA
San Bernardino, CA
12 February 2019